John F. Glaser
29 October 1962

ন/M

Elizabeth Cadbury

ELIZABETH MARY CADBURY, D.B.E., M.A., J.P.

About 1923.

Photo H. J. Whitlock and Sons, Ltd.

Fr.

ELIZABETH CADBURY
1858–1951

by

Richenda Scott

GEORGE G. HARRAP & CO. LTD
LONDON TORONTO WELLINGTON SYDNEY

First published in Great Britain 1955
by GEORGE G. HARRAP & CO. LTD
182 High Holborn, London, W.C.1

COMPOSED IN BEMBO TYPE AND PRINTED BY
MORRISON AND GIBB LIMITED, LONDON AND EDINBURGH
MADE IN GREAT BRITAIN

Contents

Illustrations

1

The Background

ELIZABETH CADBURY came of sturdy, middle-class Quaker stock, which included in its admixture both the rigidity of the Puritan and the vision of the pioneer. Merchants, industrialists, sea-faring men, and their wives of forthright character were among her ancestors, men and women who were prepared to form their own judgments of conduct, to scorn convention if necessary, and to go forward undaunted in any unpopular action which appealed to them as right.

On both sides of her family she could claim a long Quaker heritage. Through her maternal grandparents, Elizabeth Pettifer Lucas and William Cash, she could trace her descent from the early generations of the Quaker movement in the seventeenth century. One of her Lucas forebears, born in 1748, married into the family of Hayhurst, who claimed Eleanor Monk, a relative of Cromwell's great general, as a forebear. The Hayhursts joined the Society of Friends in the eighteenth century, and another member was the mother of Robert Pope, physician to George III. Through the Lucas connexion Elizabeth Cadbury was also distantly related to John Bright, the great Liberal politician and the leader of the Anti-Corn-Law agitation. John Bright's younger sister Priscilla, who became the wife of Duncan McLaren, of Edinburgh, was one of the first advocates of women's right to vote, and maintained her interest in the suffrage movement up to the year of her death in 1911.

Elizabeth Cadbury's great-grandfather on the paternal side, Henry Taylor,[1] joined the Society together with his wife shortly after their marriage in 1766. Henry Taylor spent fifteen years of his life at sea, twelve of them in command of ships carrying

[1] He was born at Whitby in 1737, and is alleged to have been a boyhood friend and playmate of Captain Cook.

merchandise. A story of him handed down in the Taylor and Cadbury families was of the great storm on New Year's Day of 1767, when Henry Taylor, with his wife on board, sailed from North Shields in company with fifteen other ships. On crossing the bar, they ran into the teeth of a northerly gale, the ship's boats were swept away, the floors of the cabins were soon awash, and the tiller finally broke. For two days and nights they drifted helplessly, but Mrs Taylor, alone in her cabin, which was ankle deep in water, with none to spare time to give attention to her, "showed no signs of fear." Of the fifteen ships setting out together only six survived those nightmare hours of storm.

Henry Taylor's chief claim to remembrance, however, is the fact that he invented or developed the idea of the 'floating light,' or lightships, of which he built and equipped two at his own expense for use off Haseboro' (Happisburgh) Gat on the Norfolk coast, and later off the Goodwin Sands, both death-traps to the seamen of his day.

His youngest son, Joseph, was the grandfather of Elizabeth Cadbury. He lived in London for some time, where her father and other sons were born, then went to Middlesborough in Yorkshire, where he was connected with the great iron works, though, like many young Friends of ability in the nineteenth century, he retired early from business. In 1807 he married Elizabeth Harris, the daughter of another master mariner, Anthony Harris, of Cumberland, whose wife was of Irish Quaker extraction. Anthony Harris was a staunch advocate of the abolition of slavery, and carried his protest into practice by refusing to wear the usual dark-blue clothing of the seaman, because the indigo used for the dye was produced by slave labour. His wife, after his death at sea, spent many years from 1803 at the Friends' School at Ackworth, looking after the girls and their teachers by helping them in the preparation of lessons and in 'their domestic habits,' and also travelling from time to time among the Quaker Meetings of the North of England.

Her daughter, Elizabeth, who married Joseph Taylor in the early nineteenth century, was the grandmother of Elizabeth Cadbury. She appears to have been an attractive and lovable woman, especially to young people, with a gift for an original ministry. A member of the Society of Friends who had met her in Darlington wrote to Dame Elizabeth in later years:

> Your grandmother was tall; an impressive figure, a shawl on her shoulders, and pure white muslin folds under her dress. . . . I have an impression of her speaking from a Psalm with a calm and distinct utterance; she had a kind concern over the youths of the Meeting, and I think was *persona grata* to the children, for they brought a puppy or two for her to admire.[1]

Elizabeth Cadbury herself recalled the long visits which this grandmother paid to her home when she was a child: "I remember her well, especially her prayers at our morning reading, the music of her voice attracting and remaining with me longer than the actual words." [2]

Joseph and Elizabeth Taylor had a large family, of whom the fourth son, John, became the father of Elizabeth Cadbury. He began his career as a member of a great engineering firm at Stockton-on-Tees, but came to London in 1853 to start in business as a stockbroker with two other Friends in the firm which became that of Fox, Taylor, and Backhouse, of 5 Tokenhouse Yard. He was a young man of Liberal views, and his farewell address to a large gathering of his friends and fellow workers before he left Stockton shows the progressive trend of his thought. For he urged the extension of educational opportunities to the working man, and spoke of the extension of the franchise "looming in the future" for which it was necessary that the workers should equip themselves. He was an enthusiast for the unpopular cause of temperance, and one of the reasons that had brought him to London was the suggestion of Samuel Bowly that he might use his gifts for that cause against the apathy or opposition of the inhabitants of the capital. Shortly after his arrival in London he was invited by the eldest son to the home of the late William Cash, a Quaker corn merchant, who had died in the cholera outbreak of 1849. At dinner John Taylor was placed next to the middle daughter of the large family of ten, and found in course

[1] Letter from Isabel Barrow to Elizabeth Cadbury, quoted in the introduction to *A Dear Memory: Pages from the Letters of Mary Jane Taylor* (pp. 15–16), by Elizabeth M. Cadbury. (Printed for private circulation, 1914.)

[2] *A Dear Memory*, p. 17.

of conversation that this girl, Mary Jane Cash, was likewise keenly interested in the temperance cause, and did much visiting among the poor of the neighbourhood. His interest was quickened, and a friendship grew out of that first meeting, which quickly ripened into love and a proposal of marriage. In 1855 the wedding took place, and in the course of the next thirteen years Mary Jane Cash bore her husband ten children,[1] of whom Elizabeth was the second. The marriage was to prove one of great happiness, rich in a community of interest and of service, preaching the gospel of temperance, aiding those in poverty, distress, and sickness, serving the Society of Friends faithfully in its meetings for worship and for discipline. Above all, they enjoyed together the task of bringing up their large and boisterous family. The shadow which lay over John Taylor's later years could never obscure for his children the memory of the father of their young days, the eager companion of long country walks who taught them the names of trees and flowers, who entered into the joys and adventures of the nursery, and gave them freedom to follow their diverse pursuits and interests.

[1] Margaret (Pearlie), 1856; Elizabeth Mary, 1858; Janet, 1859; John Howard, 1861; Wilfrid, 1863; Rosamund Isabel, 1866; Annie Frances, 1868; Josephine, 1869; Edwin Claude, 1871; John Augustine, 1873.

2

A Mid-Victorian Childhood

ELIZABETH MARY TAYLOR was born on June 24—Mid-summer Day—in the year 1858, at 3 Elm Place,[1] Peckham Rye, in the south of London. She was the second child and daughter in a family of ten, which gave her five sisters and four brothers.

Peckham, though only four miles from Charing Cross, still maintained much of the flavour of a country village. In the early years of his residence there John Taylor drove into the city daily by a coach-and-four, for there was no railway or horse-tram running through the farmlands and woods and orchards, which were as yet barely touched by the out-reaching tentacles of London.

By the time she was a year old Elsie Taylor[2] was beginning to assert herself and to show signs of a strong independence. "Baby Elsie is still a little round-about," wrote her mother to a friend, "and at a very winning age, but with a will of her own that amazes me, and makes me feel there will be some hard decisions to be arrived at as time advances"—though "she cannot run quite alone yet, and can only say one word 'Ta' . . . Pearlie [the pet name for Margaret, her older sister born in 1856] is very fond of her, but rather rough withal, but to baby Elsie this matters little; she bears all with wonderful equilibrium and seldom gets hurt in the scrambles they have together."[3]

There is another glimpse of Elsie at the age of three, so sturdy and brown and with hair so rumpled that she was easily mistaken for a boy by a visiting Friend. Her sister Margaret on the other hand was pale and slender, too delicate to walk very far, but

[1] A garage now stands on the site.
[2] Elizabeth Taylor was known throughout her childhood and girlhood as Elsie, and in later life it was the name used by her close friends and her relations.
[3] *A Dear Memory*, p. 164–165.

with the capacity of amusing herself for hours together with her toys, treating them as living things with great care "and building quite prettily with her bricks." Her patience was often sorely tried by the young Elsie, who would sweep down to destroy the house or castle wantonly; restless and active as a little bird, "she scatters her own playthings far and wide with all her might, a trick Pearlie *never* had. She *never* threw them on the floor even with intention," writes the mother, with an anxious eye on her mischievous younger daughter.[1]

Not far distant from Elm Place stood the house of Elsie Taylor's grandmother, Elizabeth Cash, where she lived with her two daughters Ann and Caroline.[2] Elsie Taylor remembered her Aunt Annie as gentle, imaginative, and sympathetic, while her Aunt Carrie was a bracing person, full of "delightful ideas and plans, and a critical faculty that stimulated effort."[3] There was a constant coming and going between the two households, and the little Taylors often spent the day with their grandmother, perhaps with their Reed cousins[4] from North London as fellow guests, playing through the summer hours in the winding walks of the garden and among its great cedar-trees, or, on wet after-noons, romping in the hall which ran through the house. The two aunts were adepts at battledore-and-shuttlecock and kept the feathered cock flying to and fro hundreds of times across the hall, or there was a game called La Crosse where a small hoop was tossed from crossed sticks to be caught across a stretch of the floor. At Christmas-time plays were anxiously rehearsed and acted under the direction of the vital and energetic Aunt Carrie, who wrote the dialogue for the children to learn. Once, while the American Civil War was raging, a freed slave was invited to the Christmas party at the last moment, bringing *Uncle Tom's Cabin* to life on the family hearth. Aunt Carrie hurriedly made a workbag as a present for his wife, so that the suddenly invited guest should not lack a gift from the Christmas tree.

[1] *A Dear Memory*, p. 169–170.
[2] Caroline later married George Barrow of Birmingham.
[3] *A Dear Memory*, p. 22.
[4] Mary Jane Taylor's sister, Selina, married Alexander Reed and had three boys and one girl.

HENRY TAYLOR
Great-grandfather.

ELIZABETH PETIPHER
(LUCAS) CASH
Grandmother.

MARY JANE (CASH)
TAYLOR
Mother.

JOHN TAYLOR
Father.

AS A GIRL (c. 1874)

AT ABOUT THE TIME
OF HER MARRIAGE
(c. 1888)

GEORGE CADBURY
(c. 1906)

ELIZABETH CADBURY
(c. 1906)

Photos Elliott and Fry

15

er sister Frances was born. Mabel, the youngest daughter of
ck and Martha Cash, married John Henry Barlow, who in
come was to act for many years as Secretary of the Bourn-
illage Trust, invited to that post by Elsie Taylor's husband,
Cadbury. The week before her marriage Elsie Taylor
Gloucester and had a long "last walk" with Uncle Fred,
a wonderful companion on a tramp across country.
Yorkshire there were many relatives from John Taylor's
f the family, offering their hospitality at holiday time to
rowing brood at Sunbury. Elsie Taylor paid a first visit
age of four to an uncle's home at Redcar, Mrs Taylor
g her three little daughters and the new baby, Howard,
at from London to the Yorkshire coast. In turn, the doors
nbury would be opened to a crowd of relatives and friends,
ially at Yearly Meeting time, the great annual gathering
e Society of Friends, when Quakers from all parts of the
sh Isles flocked to London to attend the sessions. From her
years, therefore, Elsie Taylor was aware of belonging to a
inctive Quaker clan, and learned in time to find her own
ting among them.
ummer holidays were taken *en famille*—spent at the seaside
on a farm in the country, where, in wet weather, the little
ylors were turned out, to their delight, to play barefoot in
meadows. One such holiday always stood out in the family
nals because it began with a near tragedy. A house had been
en at Shanklin, in the Isle of Wight, in 1867, when Elsie
as nine years old, and the last new baby, Isabel, a little over a
ar. A great migration took place of the parents and the six
ildren then born, a nurse, and Elsie's dog Twist. The boat
as late in getting in, and the driver of a coach or horse-omnibus
ersuaded John Taylor to accept his services in taking the party
cross the island to Shanklin. But he had been celebrating the
Queen's birthday the day before, and proved to be still incapable
f handling the horses. All the family, except the nurse, the baby,
nd the dog, were riding on top of the vehicle to enjoy the view,
when the driver missed the road altogether, set his horses at
a steep bank, and overturned the coach. The passengers were
flung into the road; John Taylor struck his head on a stone, and

Towards the end of 1863, by which time a third daughter,
Janet, and two sons, Howard and Wilfrid, had been added to
the rapidly growing family of John and Mary Jane Taylor, it
was decided to move to a larger house called Sunbury, at the
head of the Rye. It was farther from London, but stood on
higher ground than the old home, and had a considerable piece
of land attached, which was gradually transformed into a garden
by the enthusiastic botanist John Taylor. "I wish thou knew
our country view and could tell our pleasure in watching the
trees across the common coming into leaf with the fresh, sweet
green of spring, and our enjoyment in the line of gentle hills
beyond before they are spoilt with the railway embankment
that already (I am sorry to say) is fast coming on," wrote Mary
Jane Taylor to a friend in April 1864, from the new home. "I
think these multitudes of railways are becoming a great evil, I
cannot abide them," she added.[1]

Elsie Taylor was desolate at the thought of leaving Elm Place;
she took her little chair and sat down by her own rose-tree and
refused to budge! But the new house was soon discovered to
have its compensations. An old coach-house, with two rooms
above, was converted into a playroom where the children could
romp and shout to their hearts' content with no one to complain
of the noise. A vaulting-horse and spring-board were installed,
a small swing, and a ladder to climb rung by rung on the under-
side using the hands only (an exercise especially recommended
for Elsie, who had been dropped by a nursemaid in her babyhood,
leaving a doubt for some years whether or no her spine were
injured). Here, too, lived the great rocking-horse on which
five children could ride at a time, galloping to Babylon and
back before candlelight. Finally, to reconcile her to the move,
Elsie was given a Pomeranian-Esquimaux puppy, named Twist,
the son of her Aunt Carrie's dog, Hero; Twist remained a
constant companion and friend till his death when Elsie was
seventeen. "We almost lived in two big chestnut-trees and
swung ourselves almost to the sky in a very big, high swing,"
said the youngest daughter of the family, Josephine, recalling
those happy days of childhood; and Elizabeth Cadbury noted

[1] *A Dear Memory*, p. 214.

that they were all fond of walking, and were encouraged to go on long rambles, exploring the fields and meadows which lay beyond the garden where nightingales sang in the hedgerows on the June evenings, plodding up the hillside of Honor Oak, climbing trees, and racing with iron hoops "not wooden ones, and this I think taught us to run fast, as I could outrun any of my friends." Exciting games of cricket were played on the common, and a game of 'Robbers' in the garden after dark by the flickering light of a bull's-eye lantern was a favourite rough-and-tumble pastime. The roof of the house itself presented untold delights. "Janet and I used to climb up a long ladder perched on a water-butt near the stables with our dolls tied round our necks, and had great fun playing houses among the chimney-pots, and thrilling adventures in climbing from one part of the roof to another and sliding down the slopes," wrote Elizabeth Cadbury. When a neighbour, in great trepidation, appeared one day to inquire if Mary Jane Taylor knew that her daughters were on the roof, she replied calmly that unless children learned to take risks when young they were not likely to accomplish much in later life.

An innovation for that period was the introduction of a piano into this Quaker household. The Society of Friends was still held in the bonds of its Puritan heritage and regarded music and the arts as among the snares of worldliness. But a piano came to Sunbury, and the little Taylor girls learned to play upon it, and cared little for the disapproval of their conservative cousin, Priscilla Pitt, who so feared the risk of contamination that when calling at the house she would always stipulate "not in the room with the instrument, Mary Jane," when Mrs Taylor came into the hall to greet her.

From the age of five Elsie Taylor was taken to the Friends' Meeting for Worship at Peckham every Sunday, though the meeting lasted for an hour and a half and was often held largely in silence, a severe strain on an active and restless child. Peckham was an old-fashioned, comfortable meeting-house, with its bare, white-washed walls, and raised seats, occupied by Ministers and Elders, at the head of the room.

We loved listening to Grandmamm and spoke with the curious 'Plain-S . . . There were five remarkable ro feet across, I believe, which could be tion; gazing at them I am afraid I p imagining attacks of bandits or pira possessor of the secret, could rescue Fri each riding up out of reach into the ro

As the children grew older John Ta which was held for half an hour befo the Meeting for Worship. "I owe my to the interest with which he surrounde and New Testament," stated Elizabeth later. As a young woman returning fro at home, Elsie Taylor in her turn took children of the Meeting, lessening the limbs of the potential little Quakers must benches, while the minutes ticked slowly

There was a large circle of relations, in to eighty cousins in various degrees of k Elsie Taylor to encounter in those form childhood. Her mother's brother, Tom Cas Rosamund Rimmington, lived at No. 1 Th Rye, and so he and his wife were near neigh always ready with a joke and a tip for an im nephew, Aunt Rose who would take the litt in her pony carriage through Purley Woods. A near Croydon, lived a great-uncle, Samuel Luca Hannah, with whom Elsie Taylor spent many ing and learning the love of books. Joseph Ta brother, who had married her mother's sister Eli near Croydon and, later, at Dulwich; he would deep and pleasant voice, the newly published Idy his nieces and nephews. Farther afield, at Glou uncle, Frederick Goodall Cash, who had married at the age of nine Elsie Taylor spent three month

[1] *Historical Rhymes* (Postscript, p. 53), by Elizabeth M. for private circulation, 1937.)

B

was unconscious for the next twenty-four hours. Janet Taylor also suffered head injuries and was never again able to hear properly with one ear. Mrs Taylor, with a badly sprained ankle, had no time to think of her own distress while dealing with the bruised and shaken children and her unconscious husband. A passing chaise gave help, and eventually they all got to Shanklin, dazed and battered, but the oldest daughter wrote in later years that she did not know how her mother got through the next month, with a daughter and husband suffering from concussion, and a crowd of little ones to amuse and pacify.

An unsuccessful attempt was made to send Elsie Taylor with her sister Margaret to a day school, run by two Friends, but she proved too disturbing an element for these good ladies. "I found myself frequently standing on a form with my hands raised over my head as a punishment—for I knew not what," she tells us. So eventually Mrs Taylor removed both her daughters, and they were henceforth educated at home by governesses until the time came for them to go to boarding school. But the atmosphere of that home was itself probably the strongest moulding force in Elsie's education. Her mother was a widely read woman, and her father a keen politician always maintaining an interest in public affairs. Thus from very early days the Taylor children were aware, if but dimly, of the great events that were changing the outer face of the late Victorian world. When Elsie was nine years old the campaign for granting the vote to urban dwellers on a household basis was set on foot, led by her distant cousin John Bright. This meant the enfranchisement of the industrial workers, as John Taylor had foreseen many years before. She would hear her father reading the accounts of those mass meetings of the men from factory and mine, who assembled night by night on the lonely moorlands of the north to listen to John Bright, and found his oratory sweeping them to a new determination and purpose. The Franco-Prussian War broke out when Elsie was twelve, in the course of a year swinging the leadership of Europe from France to Germany. "Our children down to Isabel have taken a warm interest in sending their little contributions for the sick and wounded of both armies," wrote Mrs Taylor in September 1870, "and are now waiting to be set to work on the eighty yards of calico Papa has sent down for bandages, pillows, etc. Elsie is a warm partisan of the poor French; it is amusing to read the correspondence between her and Pearlie (now away at school); the latter believes in the Prussians." And in that same year came Forster's Education Act, the first tardy beginning of a system of public elementary education in this country, another cause for which John Taylor had pleaded a decade earlier.

So, from their earliest days, the children were conscious of a wider life beyond their doors and their immediate interests, a life which might be exciting and lit with beauty, or harsh with brutality and want, but in which they were inextricably involved and called upon to play a part. It is not surprising that, with such a background, several of that large and high-spirited family were to go forth as pioneers, with a love of venture into the unknown.

3

Schooldays and Early Youth

WHEN Elsie Taylor was thirteen years of age it was decided
to send her to school in Germany in company with her older
sister, Margaret, for Mrs Taylor had a poor opinion of the
general run of schools in England catering for "the daughters
of gentlemen." In February 1872 they set off with their father
on the three days' journey to Saxe-Meiningen. "We did not
travel by night," wrote Elizabeth Cadbury in later years, "there
being no sleepers, and stayed at Antwerp or Cologne or Frank-
furt on the way. We remained for a year at a time, Papa and
Mamma coming out after the first six months to pay us a visit
and take us for expeditions."

The school was situated in a large, rambling house in the town
of Saxe-Meiningen, and was under the direction of two principals,
Miss Trinks and Miss Meyer, both of whom had been governesses
in London. The town itself was still very primitive, with streets
unlit at night and no water laid on to the houses, so that all had
to be carried from the pumps. But it had a cultural and musical
life of its own, centring in the court of the Duke of Saxe-
Meiningen, and was representative of an older Germany with
its intense local patriotism, and its regional culture, which was
not yet swamped by the newly created Empire.

John Taylor stayed for three days with his daughters to see
them settled in before his return to England. "I have never forgotten the feeling of utter desolation as we saw his train slowly
departing from the station," said Elizabeth Cadbury when she
was nearing the end of her life.

"On our first arrival," she continued in a chapter of reminis-
cences, "we found that we were in some ways 'peculiar.' We
were Quakers, we were teetotallers, we did not go to the theatre,
and we did not dance." A large number of the girls were English,

sent out to 'finish' their education abroad, and most were the daughters of men in one or other of the Services—Army or Navy; "we had no relations in either and had been taught that all war was wrong! We wrote home to say that we really could not carry so many 'virtues' on our young shoulders, and what could they let us off! The parents agreed that we might learn dancing. Oh, what a joy it was to join with the others in those lessons and rhythmic exercises. I can still hear the twang of the violins as we entered the Salle-de-dance." But the prohibition on attendance at the theatre or the opera remained, though Elsie protested unavailingly against it. A letter from her mother, dated October 11, 1872, and addressed to the two girls, complains, "Elsie has taken chiefly to *begging* letters, but to her last request [to attend the theatre] we give a very decided and unswerving negative! If every one in the house goes to the theatre but you, you may not. Papa said, 'Why, they will be asking to give up their teetotalism next, and because we gave leave for a few dancing lessons they seem to think we shall stand by no principles.'" In November an opportunity to go to the opera arose, and, still not disheartened by the previous stern refusal, Elsie Taylor again sent an imploring letter to her father: "Please, the very instant you read this, please take a pen and paper and write and say we may go. . . . I am sure almost you will let us, because you are so fond of music yourself, so you will sympathize with me. . . . I think you'll let us go too, because you let us go to concerts and it's very much like a concert, oh, *please* let us go."

More gently than her mother, John Taylor replied to this impassioned appeal:

I am sorry to disappoint thee in not being able to grant thy request and hope thou will accept the disappointment with a good grace. . . . Thy argument that the opera is only a little more than a concert conceals a fatal objection. For if the opera is only a little more than a concert then something else will only be a little more or nothing more than the opera, and thus the whole round of objectionable amusements will be reached. The influences of the Theatre are not for good and this in a way thou cannot fully understand; but thou can understand that it is hurtful and often ruinous to those employed and we are not to encourage a system which is attended with so much peril to those who minister to other people's pleasure or amusement. . . . A word to the wise is sufficient and I shall trust to thy being wise enough to see that for thy own good and as my daughter thou must cheerfully abstain from the theatre and opera.

Very dear love from thy ever affect:
PAPA

So, as the other girls trooped off gaily to an evening's entertainment, the two sisters were left alone with one lamp in a corner of the big schoolroom. It was a severe test of conscience, when the creaking wooden verandas that ran at three levels round the quadrangle suggested the approach of stealthy footsteps, and the lamp made but a small pool of light and comfort beyond which stretched the shadows, where strange dangers might lurk to an imaginative child. Certainly there were moments when Elsie rebelled against the fate which had made her a Quaker, as she frankly confesses. She doubtless suffered much from the self-conscious difficulty of being different from the crowd, that difference which can so haunt a girl in her teens when her desire is to mingle and blend with her contemporaries, to be one wholly of the group in which she lives.

Looking back on these experiences in the latter years of her life, however, Dame Elizabeth Cadbury felt that on the whole it had been good to face these tests, to stand for principles which, if not strictly speaking hers, were those of her family and of her religious allegiance. Gradually the differences were accepted by her schoolfellows; she made friends, and entered into the routine, the mischief, and the work of her new school life. The lessons in history and literature, given by a German professor, stood out in her memory; and "England slipped into her place as being one amongst others of the European countries"—a member of the European civilization—and this perspective was to prove an inestimable advantage to Elizabeth Cadbury in her later international work and interests. But the great joy and benefit of this time in Germany was the opportunity of hearing and learning really good music. "We had an excellent teacher, Herr Hockstein. The Duke of Meiningen was a patron of both

music and the drama and we regularly attended concerts and
became familiar with the works of Haydn, Beethoven, Bach,
Mozart, and many others."

Half-holidays were spent on the hills outside the town where
the headmistress had an old house, once an inn, surrounded by a
large garden. There was a spacious hall with a stage on which
the girls acted German plays. "On the outskirts of the town and
through the woods flowed a river in which we bathed, and down
which floated great rafts of trees felled in the vast Thuringian
forest. The weather was very cold in the winter; it was possible
to skate for at least two months, and we were allowed to skate
on the lake in the Duke's park." The Duke would walk round
with his greyhounds, and on special occasions his regimental
band was in attendance, playing in the frosty stillness.

Several of the daughters of families connected with the Court
came to the school for lessons in French and English, and the
pupils from overseas were sometimes invited to their houses.
Elsie Taylor was popular, and enjoyed the hospitality of the
small German nobility of Saxe-Meiningen on many occasions.
There were walks in the spring and summer through the great
forest, sometimes to a castle three miles away where Queen
Victoria had once stayed and where coffee or lager beer could
be obtained at a little *Wirtshaus*. And occasionally there were
longer excursions to Eisenach or Coburg or Liebenstein.

Elsie Taylor, though interested in much of her work, was
anything but a model pupil. There was a constant battle with
untidiness; there was rebellion against the petty discipline of
apparently unnecessary rules. In her first term sixteen good
marks were earned, as against twenty bad ones—the highest
number of bad marks given to any girl that quarter—and her
school reports made sad reading!

Her difficulties, her successes and punishments, are all detailed
with the utmost candour in the letters to her parents; there is
no attempt to hide anything. The warm, impetuous nature of
the girl is revealed in those untidily scrawled pages which her
father claims he can only read with the greatest difficulty. Why,
oh, why, can she not emulate the neatness of her model elder
sister?

Her last year at the school Elsie thoroughly enjoyed, perhaps in part because that older sister was removed, to return home and help her mother with the new baby, John Augustine, born in November 1873. On July 15, 1874, Elsie herself came back to London to complete her education there. Her homecoming was shadowed by the death of her little sister Isabel after only a week or two's illness, the first experience of that great rift within her near circle.

In the autumn of that year Elsie entered the North London Collegiate School, where she was a pupil for the next two years, under the headship of the great pioneer of women's education, Miss Buss. The school had been opened in 1850 as the first public school for girls in the country, providing for the daughters of the middle-class citizens some of the advantages which their sons enjoyed at St Paul's, Westminster, or Harrow. Elsie found her new headmistress a stimulating teacher; her tireless energy and enthusiasm struck a ready spark of response in the young pupil. Miss Buss, sweeping into a classroom with the sudden question, "Well, girls, what are we here for?" brushing aside the answer of learning the particular lesson of the moment with an impatient "No, no—what is the purpose behind our work?" remained a vivid memory to Elizabeth Cadbury at ninety. Deeply impressed upon her at sixteen was the realization that the higher education in which she was sharing was to fit her for a wider service to her fellows in the years to come.

While at the North London Collegiate School Elsie lived during the week with her uncle Alexander Reed, who had been widowed shortly before, and his daughter Bessie, in their home at Tufnell Park, which was not far distant from the school in Camden Road. She returned to Sunbury for week-ends, but much enjoyed her time in her uncle's house; her cousins Harry, William, and Frank Reed were frequently at home, and once more Elsie found herself a member of a lively and stimulating household.

Even the walk to school was a source of enjoyment, as the girl, with her growing interest in people, speculated on the different lives of those she encountered, or vied with them in racing along the pavements. In an essay entitled "The Walk to School" she wrote:

> Then coming into Camden Road we meet numbers of other girls coming to school, and gentlemen going to town. The latter are nearly always in a tremendous hurry, and go racing along to catch the train. Sometimes, if I am in a hurry and alone, I run races with these gentlemen, though of course only known to myself. Sometimes they win, but generally I do ! There is one that I generally pick out for these races. He looks so exceedingly proud, and runs in such a consequential manner, with his head high in the air, as though treading on all his inferiors, that I feel quite excited when I beat him, only the worst of it is that he is not aware of the fact.

Altogether she thoroughly enjoyed those last years of her school life. There was no longer rebellion against discipline; her reports were consistently satisfactory, and the teaching was excellent. For the first time she embarked upon Latin and Mathematics, which were not included in the curriculum at Saxe-Meiningen; her knowledge of French and German acquired there gained her a high place in these subjects; she was a senior girl and accepted gladly the responsibilities of that position. Shortly before leaving school in the spring of 1876 she successfully passed the Senior Cambridge Examination in ten subjects. The Cambridge Local Examinations had been opened to girls in 1865, another important stage in the raising of the standard of women's education.

In 1950 Dame Elizabeth Cadbury was a guest of honour at the dinner given to commemorate the centenary of the foundation of the North London Collegiate School, one of the very few present who had attended as a pupil of the founder and had been taught by her.

So, in the mild spring days of 1876, Elsie returned to her home at Sunbury, no longer a schoolgirl, but a young woman of nearly eighteen years, to take her place in the activities and interests of the large home circle. But first, as was often the custom in Quaker families, a round of visits was paid to their many relations by Margaret and Elsie, so that for three months they were travelling from house to house, chiefly in the north of England, making many new and lifelong friends among their cousins.

A younger sister's memories of Elsie's coming back to settle down again at home is of a new focus of liveliness and interest within the household. She was always planning things for her younger brothers and sisters to do—games, plays, picnics; she was a tireless, active, eager companion, ever ready to embark upon new interests, and entering with zest and verve into everything she undertook. There were also many opportunities to continue her education, of which she eagerly availed herself. She was a regular attender at various courses organized by London University, and went frequently to lectures at the London Institution, where she several times heard Ruskin speak. She studied in the Reading Room of the British Museum, and best of all was the opportunity to continue her music lessons at the Crystal Palace, where there was a branch of the South Kensington Institute, and to take singing lessons at the Guildhall School of Music. Her teacher was the well-known musician and exponent, Ernst Pauer; she also learned to play the organ, a joy which continued to the last weeks of her life, and she was free to practise in two neighbouring churches; her young brothers would go with her to blow the bellows and earned many coppers for this service. Every three years a Handel festival was held at the Crystal Palace, regularly attended by the Taylor girls, and proved a veritable "orgy of music" in Elizabeth Cadbury's words.

Shortly after her return from the round of family visits a governess who had lived at Sunbury for several years, teaching the younger Taylors, was obliged to return home suddenly. Elsie at once offered to fill the gap. Critical relatives remarked that the enthusiasm for this task would not last, and that the instruction given would certainly be amateur and spasmodic. "That, of course, put one on one's mettle, and my mother heartily encouraged the idea."

Her pupils were her little sisters Frances and Josephine, her brother Claude, and, later, the youngest child, John Augustine, and a small cousin, Una Taylor. She devised many ways of enlivening the lesson hours. The little girls she taught to count while practising on the piano by pulling their pig-tails, and she compiled a book of historical rhymes to lighten the memorization of dates and events. They were recited to a musical chant with rhythmic exercises, "the Swiss and the Spanish especially going with a swing," and names and dates were thereby fixed indelibly in a child's memory.

Both the teacher and her pupils thoroughly enjoyed this experiment in home education, which continued till the girls went to boarding school at Southport and Claude to King's College School in London. "I believe I should not have cared for history as much as I do if it had not been for you, we used to have such joly lessons," wrote her little brother John when he in turn had gone away to school, and the children found that they were so well grounded that they could easily hold their own with their fellow pupils in the new classrooms.

4

Life in London

THE Victorian young woman of the middle-classes, if she were not content to pass her days in a round of trivial social activities and housework, had one main outlet for her energies—the fashionable craze for 'slumming.' But, with Elsie Taylor, her efforts in this direction were based on something deeper than the patronage of the poor which helped to salve the conscience of the less thoughtful. She was growing up in an age of concentrated energy, of restless thought, of growing capacity to control and bend the forces of nature to the will of man. The expanding industrialism of the early nineteenth century, bringing in its wake new social problems of health and overcrowding, of the provision of houses for a rapidly multiplying class of factory workers, provoked in its turn a more sensitive conscience towards distress and discontent. The witness to that awakening lies in the Reports of the Royal Commissions of Enquiry of the 1830's, 1840's, and 1850's, which have been described recently as one of the glories of the early Victorian age.[1] No one growing up in the household of John and Mary Jane Taylor could be unaware of those problems, could burke what Carlyle termed "the condition of England question."

The Society of Friends at that time was very strongly swayed by the Evangelical Movement. There was a deep cleavage of thought between a conservative section, who clung to the traditional behaviour and practices of Quakerism, and still maintained a quietist pattern of mysticism in their worship and in their attitude towards life, and those who, braced with the tense enthusiasm of the converted, were fired to carry that message of salvation to all and sundry and so to multiply the number of God's elect.

[1] T. S. Ashton, in *Capitalism and the Historians* (1954), p. 35.

The desire of the quietist group was to hold aloof from the dust and dross of political strife, to preserve an inward seclusion and peace in the midst of the world's restless activity, to empty the frail human vessel so far as might be of emotion and thought, that into the purged heart and mind might be spoken the word of the Living God. The Evangelical Friend, with his passion to convert and reform, was prepared to enter the field of political activity, to take part in or initiate public philanthropic movements, such as the campaign for the abolition of slavery, for the suppression of the opium traffic with China, for stamping out drunkenness and immorality, for bringing relief to the victims of unemployment or of war. He was prepared to assume the responsibilities of local government and to seek a place as a Liberal candidate in the national Parliament. Even the sanctities of the Quaker method of worship and its peculiar forms of organization he was prepared to see modified in his effort to appeal to his unregenerate fellow-men beyond the Quaker fold, and to work, as he believed, more efficiently for them. Thus the practice grew up of holding evening meetings, not on the basis of silent worship, but with a set address of an emotional or impassioned character, accompanied by rousing hymns, vocal prayer, and Bible readings, which might attract the spiritually hungry among the working classes. Thus, too, came the growth of the Committee system within the Society, Friends of like mind banding together in groups, which were at first no official part of the Quaker organization, to raise the funds and support the workers who were carrying out their plan of campaign in the Temperance Cause, in the Foreign and Home Mission Fields, or in relief work.

Elizabeth Taylor's parents were ardent members of the Evangelical group of Friends, and her father became the first Secretary of the Friends' Temperance Union, formed in 1852. At about the time she was leaving school several members of Peckham Meeting, many of them younger people filled with the Evangelical fervour, rented two of the lofty arches of the London, Chatham, and Dover railway, bricked them up, and turned them into two large halls with adjoining classrooms. In one of the halls a service, or "Mission," meeting was conducted every Sunday evening by John Taylor, his elder daughters taking it in turns to play the harmonium and lead the singing of the hymns. A Sunday school for the young ragamuffins of the neighbourhood was held on Sunday afternoons, and Elsie was called upon to take charge of one of the classes, at first a class of little girls, and then one of small boys, but finally she settled down with a class of older boys from twelve to fifteen years of age, and numbering between thirty and forty members. They were a tough and unruly crowd for a girl to tackle; there are frequent references in Elsie's diaries to their obstreperousness and the battles she had to fight. But she wrestled valiantly with the problem, and eventually learned to win the allegiance of the changing generations of boys without difficulty. It was unusual, to say the least of it, for a young woman in the late 'teens or early twenties to take a little crowd of street arabs rowing on the lake in Battersea Park, teaching them to handle a boat, or to carry them off for tramps and explorations in the country, or to play cricket with them on the Rye, taking her turn at the wicket and batting strongly against the most stalwart bowler. But these surprising activities are an early indication of how often Elsie was to be found in the vanguard of the thought of her age; it was by such methods that she won the confidence and affection of the boys, and so could claim their attention on Sunday for her Bible lessons. She also formed a choir from their numbers which gave many entertainments, and among her cherished possessions in her home at Birmingham was a photograph of the class which the boys gave her when she left London in 1888 to marry George Cadbury.[1]

Among the new enterprises started under the impetus of the Evangelical movement by Friends were a number of mission centres in the East End of London for religious and educational purposes. At one of these in Bunhill Fields, close by the burial-place of George Fox, Mrs George Gillett, a well-known Friend, had organized various classes and an adult school for the women

---

[1] Her sister Frances carried on the class when she left. "From many of them I have heard occasionally," wrote Dame Elizabeth Cadbury in 1940, "and even as lately as 1934, when the King graciously gave me the D.B.E., I had letters of congratulation from two of my old boys."

and mothers of the neighbourhood, and enlisted the help of
Elsie Taylor in this work. She would give occasional talks on
health and hygiene or some current topic to these gatherings of
working women, learning at the same time as she tried to share
her knowledge with them. Also, as a rather daring venture,
frowned upon by some of the stricter Friends, Elsie organized
a choir and orchestra among them which gave many concerts.

In the year 1884, when Moody and Sankey visited London
with their fervent religious appeal, Elsie was swept into the full
flood of the Evangelical Movement. All classes in the capital
were caught up in this campaign; thousands flocked nightly to
the great halls and marquees in which the meetings were held to
hear the one preach and the other sing, and enthusiasm was
raised to fever pitch by their stirring emotional appeal. A large
choir was formed to lead the singing at these mass meetings,
of which both Margaret and Elsie Taylor were members. It
was in this choir that the latter met another life-long friend, Lily
Davey. The two young women would escape from the tense
atmosphere of the prayer-meetings which were held for the
choir before public services, to read Green's *History of the English
People* together. On one or two occasions, when Ira D. Sankey
was indisposed or tired, Elsie was asked to replace him at the
organ, and never forgot the thrill it gave her to accompany the
singing of the huge choir and the thousands of voices from the
crowd below. "The message of the two evangelists not only
laid emphasis on Belief, as did all Evangelical preachers of the
day, but also on Life—what you were, and what you did, being
more important than what you could say about it," wrote
Elizabeth Cadbury many years later.

The simplicity of their appeal, and the directness of their attack
attracted young people; at any rate they crowded into the meetings. The seven Cambridge undergraduates, who at the close of
the London campaign volunteered for foreign missionary service,
were examples of the type of youth influenced by these men.
The best known probably were the Studd brothers, Charlie and
Jack, both first-class cricketers, and Montague Beauchamp. They
all offered for China, Charlie Studd afterwards going to Central
Africa. Some years later Jack Studd (generally known as Sir

Kynaston) returned to London and became Lord Mayor, interesting himself particularly in the welfare of young men in London. The father of the Studds, who was very keen on racing and breeding horses, became a staunch supporter of the Evangelists.

The urge to be doing something became yet more of an incentive to the young and active, and Elsie was soon looking for new forms of practical service.

A first venture was to start a Boys' Club in the Ratcliffe Highway on a week-day evening, a pioneer task for a young woman of her age. Once again, as in her Sunday-school class, the young woman of twenty-six was called upon to face a crowd of unruly young barbarians from some of the poorest and roughest quarters of the dockside. Once again she managed to win and hold them by her own high-spirited, lively interest in their activities, and in themselves as human beings.

Also situated on the Ratcliffe Highway was a club for sailors from the neighbouring docks, known as "The Sailors' Rest," where Elsie was much in demand to help in entertaining the seamen of all nationalities gathered there. She taught them to play various musical instruments, or accompanied their songs, or read aloud, and generally enlivened the proceedings. Through this connexion she became interested in a Scandinavian Sailors' Home, run by Agnes Hedenstrom, a Swedish lady who had come over from Stockholm with a concern to befriend the Scandinavian sailors in the port of London, where they would often have to stay for weeks at a time. Lonely and unable to speak English, they had nowhere to go but the public-house or the brothel. Agnes Hedenstrom, together with a Swedish business-man, Axel Welin, who was representing his firm in London, set to work to provide accommodation for these men in their leisure hours. "Two or three fine old houses, dating no doubt from the time when the proximity of the Thames made them summer resorts, were their first headquarters and were used as a hostel for thirty or forty sailors," wrote Elizabeth Cadbury.

Eventually a splendid new Home was built in the East India Docks, and there I helped Miss Hedenstrom to entertain King Oscar of Sweden who came to open it. Hundreds of Scandinavians

C

must have passed through its doors and found fellowship there. We found King Oscar a delightful person, cheery and friendly, and on excellent terms with his sailors.

I think Miss Hedenstrom was the most devoted worker that I have ever known. She lived amongst the sailor folk and was at their service day and night. When a big Scandinavian boat arrived she would go down to the docks while the sailors were being discharged and paid off, in order to save them from the harpies who always awaited the arrival of a ship, and after she would bring to the Home for shelter stranded seamen, or families migrating to other parts. Two or three times I stayed for the night when helping her. On one occasion a Finnish woman and her three children, on their way to America, shared my tiny room with me; for Miss Hedenstrom that sort of thing was a frequent occurrence. It was most difficult to persuade her to take a holiday, but once she entrusted me to take charge while she had two days off; an exciting experience for me!

Agnes Hedenstrom and Axel Welin were eventually married, but not for some time after the opening of the Home; "they said that they were too busy to think of it before!"

Elsie, with a number of other young women of leisure, as she tells us, "by way of making friends with girls who worked in shops, offices, warehouses, etc., undertook, with the approval of the employers, to pay visits once a week during the lunch-hour, taking flowers and giving talks to the girls while they ate their sandwiches and had cups of tea or coffee brought to them." Elsie's particular haunt was a publishing firm in Paternoster Row with some sixty to seventy employees.

My girls and I became very good friends. They bought a little harmonium to help the music, as they loved singing hymns. I remember that some would ask, with a grin, for one of Sankey's entitled 'Where is my wandering boy to-night' . . . We had quite a sad parting when I married, and I continued my visits until a week before my wedding day, when I left with them a cake to be enjoyed on the right date.

In February 1885 Elsie was invited to join for a time a Protestant mission in Paris, presided over by Mademoiselle de Broen, and in which Friends were much interested. The mission had grown

out of the relief brought by English Friends to the victims of the
Franco-Prussian War. An orphanage was opened, originally for
children whose parents had died in the conflict, and medical
aid was given freely to the poor of the city. There were many
voluntary helpers, visiting the homes of those seeking relief
and dispensing medicines for the sick, and, as part of the treatment, giving instruction in the Evangelical faith to the hapless
patients. The mission was situated in a large house in Belleville—
the Communist quarter of Paris, as Elsie describes it—and the
inhabitants of the surrounding tenements flocked to the dispensary, including among their numbers French, German,
Italian, Flemish, and Dutch. "There are a good many Germans
in Paris and they all fall to my lot as I am the only one here
who can speak German," Elsie wrote home in a letter to her
mother. "It is computed that in this quarter of Paris alone 15,000
men are out of work, so, in visiting our patients in their homes,
it is *intensely* sad to see the utter poverty to which they are
reduced." During her time in Paris Elsie witnessed the anniversary
of the inauguration of the French Republic "when all Paris
turned out to enjoy themselves." She was also among the crowds
who visited the coffin of Victor Hugo lying in state at the Arc de
Triomphe.

On her return to London in July of 1885, she tells us that after
seeing the homes of the street-sweepers and rag-and-bone merchants in Paris "who lived in a *quartier* by themselves, in hovels
surrounded by a wall," she was determined to learn more of the
social conditions in her own capital. So she began a regular
visitation in the slums that lay near Bunhill, Shoreditch, and
Ratcliff, and learned how the poor of London lived. She was
filled with a bitter indignation against the landlords of slum
property; as she paced the muddy streets of the East End the
question as to whence arose the surrounding poverty, how it was
to be combated and overcome, hammered persistently in her
brain. It was to continue, an unceasing query, to the end of her
life. For to her there was no facile answer in the current ideologies
propounded by the varying generations she saw come and go.
Was it sufficient even to trust to the slow enlightenment of public
opinion, pressing measures of reform upon the government?

"I dislike all societies and assemblies of men and distrust their powers of effecting thoroughly what they determine, with however good intentions they may start," she wrote in 1883 in an essay on poverty read to a Quaker literary and debating circle, the Portfolio Society. "Much time, money and patience are recklessly lost, and the comparative results poor. Most good done in the world is by individual effort." She felt that it was particularly the right and the work of woman "to raise mankind from the degrading depths to which it has fallen." Her immediate practical suggestion was that a number of concerned women should take a room apiece in different parts of the East End, furnish these dwelling-places tastefully and simply, and by living among and identifying themselves with the people come to win their friendship and confidence. Lessons in cooking, dress-making, in reading and writing, were to be given in these rooms to the women living within a quarter-of-a-mile radius, and lectures on the laws of health and on other "useful subjects." Saturdays were to be devoted to real games—cricket, tennis, football—played on the large open spaces left in the middle of London's new model buildings. The evenings were to be given to classes for men, and the children, after school, were to be gathered and taught to play organized games instead of haunting the streets as wayward hooligans. Elsie was aware that some institutions had began work of this nature, "but what I want is to concentrate in one spot and carry on these efforts right in the homes of the poor," she writes, and she would like her "reformers" established in every quarter of a square mile in London.

This paper attracted the attention of a young man, Edward Pease, who was present at the Portfolio Meeting, and a correspondence sprang up between the two and was continued at intervals over the next few years. Edward Pease, who was later to become a well-known public figure as the secretary of the Fabian Society, had obviously taken a prominent part in the Portfolio discussions at Cavendish Square, and a few days later Elsie flung aside convention, and wrote frankly to him:

I have been meditating for some days sending you a line or two, being wishful of expressing an idea or so, and have come to the conclusion that I am sufficiently revolutionary to be careless of conventionalities and to do as I please.

It was the receipt of that poem and also various remarks of yours the other night at Cavendish Square that determined me. . . . What seems to me wrong about all these socialist reforms is first, that the day is always *coming*, people of the future will have the benefit if it comes at all, but those of the present who require help, they have to listen to lectures and poems, and their present pressing need is untouched. *That* is looked after by philanthropists at whom and whose beliefs the revolutionists scoff.

Already, at twenty-five, it was the immediate, practical steps, the piece of work to be done here and now, that appealed to Elsie rather than any doctrine of human rights or dreams of a social Utopia. And that was to remain true throughout the years ahead.

She herself was at this time anxious to carry out her project of living in the East End, but was finally prevented by the claims of her home and her parents. It was a dream that died hard. She was a reader of Carlyle, and must have realized, with him, that the middle- and upper-classes confronted with the social problem of that age were being led "to the shore of a boundless continent . . . lying huge, dark, unexplored, inevitable," which they must enter perforce and find a way through, step by step, for "one way or another there must be a solution."[1]

Edward Pease and a circle of his friends were drawn to Russian Nihilism—as their counterparts of the present day find certain affinities with Russian Communism. He was therefore breaking with his Quaker faith, and announced himself in a letter to Elsie as an agnostic and a revolutionist. It is in her reply to this letter that she speaks most frankly of her own conflict with doubt. She had read the *Origin of Species* (published in the year after her birth) when she was in her early twenties; she was conversant with the prevailing doctrine of determinism—the view that man as a biological species is imprisoned in a mechanical

[1] Thomas Carlyle, *Essay on Chartism* (Everyman Edition of Carlyle's Essays, 1940, Vol. II, p. 206).

universe, that consciousness, thoughts, and feelings as well as bone and sinew belong entirely to the natural order, that man, in short, had been thrust rudely from his place as the unique creation of the Godhead to be plunged, body and spirit, back into the stream of nature.

"Most of us were more or less affected by the scepticism and agnosticism then prevalent," wrote a contemporary of Elizabeth Cadbury, Helen M. Sturge, of Bristol, who was born in the same year, and who came likewise from an old Quaker family. "Those were the days of Professor T. H. Huxley and Professor Tyndall and Herbert Spencer, whose criticism was almost entirely destructive. There was very little help for us. To-day, although doubt and scepticism are still active, there is very much more constructive help for young people."[1]

Elsie, in the letter to Edward Pease from which extracts have already been quoted, says:

> You said (in the discussion at Cavendish Square), "I fear I have ceased to believe in the old way," and I took the "old way" to mean our religion. I suppose in the "new life" people may speak or write unreservedly, the contrary seeming to me a bad system, and of course everything then will be perfect, so I am just anticipating that time, and trust I am not doing wrong, or making matters worse to you, which fear preventing [prevented?] my touching on such a subject before.
>
> I wanted to say that with anyone who had felt doubts as to the efficacy of the "old way," I felt the keenest sympathy, for I cannot tell you all I have passed through on that point myself. Don't think me given to exaggeration or strong language, but I believe I would almost rather die than pass through a certain six months of my life not so very long ago, again. It seemed all utterly impossible. I had been studying physiology and reading German philosophy, so I do not speak without knowing the grounds of dispute. I cannot say that these thoughts (and doubts) do not return occasionally now, but as I decided once firmly, after great consideration, they do not trouble so much, though they make me utterly wretched. Yet I feel I have come safely through the waters on to dry land, and by God's grace I will keep there.

---

[1] "Centenary Chapters," in *The Friend*, March 5, 1943, p. 169.

It is her only surviving reference to this dark period of her life, though some of her correspondents refer to difficulties which must have been mentioned in letters to them.

The decisive factor which helped finally to resolve many of her doubts was not intellectual but practical. Wrestling with her difficulties, repelled by the narrowness and intolerance of much organized religion of her day, disturbed and baffled by the new thought and its threat to old beliefs, she was content to cherish the flickering light that was vouchsafed to her, and, starting from that, she found fresh strength coming to reinforce her experience of God. As she moved among the harsh realities of slum life and encountered its brutalized inhabitants she found presently that she could "speak from the heart" of truths that she had hitherto accepted intellectually. It was the power of the Christian experience to lift a man or woman into a larger life, to remould anew some of his most repellent features, that gave her back her own faith in its fullness. "It was the effect of Christianity that dragged me back to it," she told Edward Pease. But those months of doubt and despair were never forgotten, and were always to give her a particular sympathy with youth and its difficulties.

The imagination of Elsie Taylor was presently caught by the "brave music of a distant drum" as she looked about her restlessly in these years, where the needs and claims of her fellowmen met her on every side. In the spring of 1883 she heard from a friend of hers in Ceylon, who was working with the Church Missionary Society, that there was likely to be a vacancy in about a year's time for an English teacher in a Tamil girls' boarding-school. This correspondent was sure that the life and work would suit Elsie Taylor exactly, but mentions that it would be well for her to be confirmed before offering herself to the C.M.S. It is possible that this letter first put the thought of confirmation into her mind. For some time past she had been in the habit of practising the organ in a neighbouring church, and sometimes played for the services, so that she had become more familiar with the Anglican liturgy than was the case with many Friends. The dignity and beauty of the language, the undying nature of the experience embodied in prayers and collects, even the clear-cut confession of faith in the Nicene creed, all made a strong appeal to her. In the autumn of 1886, after many talks with Mrs Graham at Sandown, the mother of her school friend Edith, Elsie was baptized into the Church of England while staying in the Isle of Wight. She did not resign her membership in the Society of Friends, and it is doubtful if many, outside her immediate family, knew of the step she had taken. Attendance at church and at the Communion lasted only for a short period thereafter, for in the following year she met again the man who was to become her future husband, and in his staunch and unquestioning faith she found the answer to many problems and the anchorage of a creed was no longer necessary to her.

Life was by no means entirely occupied with 'good works' and intellectual wrestling. Elsie Taylor was a leader among the group of young Friends in London, planning long days on the river or country rambles and picnics, arguing, talking, laughing. She was a member of various Quaker reading circles and debating societies, and herself organized one such group for political discussion among her young women compatriots, as the older Friends in the more orthodox Quaker circles considered that only men were qualified to take part in political debates. In one of these societies she persuaded some of her contemporaries to join with her in the production of Browning's *Colombe's Birthday* —a most successful performance, which caused a minor storm among the older Friends, who were shocked at the very thought of amateur theatricals. But a love of acting was inborn with Elsie, and found an outlet at the least opportunity. She was also a keen tennis player, loved walking and driving, sailing and swimming, and plunged into whatever she did with the same infectious enthusiasm.

The meetings of the Portfolio Society were frequently held at the house of Jonathan Hutchinson, the surgeon, in Cavendish Square; his daughter Elsie was a very great friend of Elizabeth Taylor's. The Hutchinsons and a small group, of which Elsie Taylor was one, produced a quarterly magazine called the *Hoi-Polloi*, to which all kinds of people contributed, and which included in its pages sketches and pen-and-ink drawings.

Elsie Hutchinson, the editor, kept it going for a long time;

and Ethel,[1] her sister, contributed many charming water-colour sketches. Elsie Hutchinson later married Thomas P. Newman, a member of Peckham Meeting. Elizabeth Cadbury liked to recall the delightful evenings spent at Cavendish Square, and summer visits to Haslemere,[2] when music, sketching, Browning readings, and all sorts of games filled the hours. Jonathan Hutchinson was a man of wide sympathies and with a richly stored mind; his wife was artistic, musical, and very attractive. Elsie Taylor first heard Browning's poem *Saul* read aloud by Jonathan Hutchinson one evening, an experience she never forgot.

Most enjoyable of all were the informal gatherings at Sunbury, when the sons and daughters brought home their friends for an evening of music and singing, and of reading aloud, each taking some character part impromptu, or acting together charades or hastily contrived plays.

Elsie's holidays, too, were often unorthodox and certainly invigorating. "When I was twenty," says Dame Elizabeth, "Margaret, Janet (who was eighteen), and I, with a friend of Margaret's, Lydia Whitehead, enjoyed a walking tour in the Lake district. Mama was criticised for allowing this rather unusual venture, but it was a great success." The four girls travelled all night from London to Penrith (they probably travelled third class), arriving at 5.0 A.M. Like any modern hiker they shouldered their knapsacks, walked five miles to Ullswater, and after breakfast at an inn rowed the length of the lake, nine miles in all, to Patterdale. Here a guide urged them to climb Helvellyn if they wished for a view, as he prophesied rain for the next day; so after lunch they set off again, climbed the mountain, and had magnificent views. This was merely the prelude to a strenuous fortnight of exploration.

[1] She became Ethel Chandler.

[2] Jonathan Hutchinson discovered and developed the land in Surrey now the well-known health resort of Haslemere. The family had a summer cottage there; in 1885, after her return from Paris, Elsie Taylor with her sisters, Frances and Josephine, and her young brothers, Claude and Jack, took a cottage near by and enjoyed doing everything for themselves "except cleaning saucepans and preparing game"; this a neighbouring cottager undertook. "One of our happiest experiences," says Elsie, "was entertaining our mother one week-end and our father the next."

In the summer of 1883 her aunt and uncle, Caroline and George Barrow, took Elsie with a party of young people to Switzerland —"five interesting individuals, the Rector, the Poetess, the Artist, the Philosopher, and the Musician," her diary notes. And the sketches it contains brings before us those "interesting individuals" in their tight Victorian dresses with puffed sleeves, wide-brimmed hats, stove-pipe trousers, and straw 'boaters,' rowing on the Lake of Lucerne, glissading perilously in long skirts and nipped-in jackets down the snow slopes of the Rücken Pass, or navigating a glacier roped to their guides.

Another holiday, organized by the same aunt and uncle, was certainly a novel one for that day (1886). They chartered a wherry on the Norfolk Broads, and took a party of their nephews, nieces, and their friends exploring the inland waterways, which were then empty of holiday craft. Elsie and Janet Taylor insisted on sleeping in a tent on shore on some nights to escape from their cramped quarters on board, a departure which caused consternation to their aunt, who appeared when they were in bed to fasten the tent flap firmly with a safety-pin as a protection against all night prowlers.

Elsie also maintained a close friendship with one of her old schoolfellows of Saxe-Meiningen, Edith Graham, whose home was in the Isle of Wight, and several holidays were spent there. Elsie became a member of the crew of the Graham's yacht, the *Wonga-Wonga*, and joined Edith Graham and her brothers in sailing round the island. Sometimes the boat was manned entirely by the two girls and their friends; "if we got into difficulties there was always a yacht full of young men about, who would come to lend us a hand," said Dame Elizabeth, recalling those carefree days.

Certainly, her life at this time was a strenuous one, but she had the capacity to seize every moment of the crowded days and to live them with zest to the full. There was a great attraction about the plain, eager girl with her ringing laugh, her ready wit, her boundless energy; young men and women found delight in her companionship, looked to her for ideas to fill their leisure hours, and followed her lead with enjoyment.

In the spring and summer of 1886 plans were made for another migration of the Taylor family to a new and larger house. "We had so often talked of moving from 'the Rye,' " wrote Elizabeth Cadbury in a footnote to one of her mother's published letters,

and at last had found a house we liked [at 208 Denmark Hill], not too far from the old Meeting to prevent our still attending. It was the Friends' Meeting that really kept us in the neighbourhood. Our friends had practically all left that part of London, and we disliked our surroundings. . . . When the time for the decision came, the thought would intrude: "Ought we to forsake the Meeting, the schools, the mission and temperance work in which we had been interested?" And with a sigh we would settle down again. But at last we had really decided on a change, though the new house was still to be in the south of London.

Mary Jane Taylor was ill for several months that winter, often suffering much pain. But her daughter Janet, who was a trained nurse, had become engaged in the spring to Joseph Henry Clark, of Doncaster, and her wedding was fixed for February of 1887. So Mrs Taylor hid her condition from her family so far as might be, and went steadily ahead with plans both for the wedding and the removal to the new home, though she must have realized as the wedding day approached that the shadows were closing about her. For the last two or three weeks before her marriage Janet was in constant attendance, nursing her mother with all the powers of her unfailing skill. Mrs Taylor was unable to attend the wedding itself, but came down to the lunch held at Sunbury beforehand. Appropriate mottoes were written out for all the guests on the name-cards marking their places. On Mary Jane Taylor's card were the words: "Her children arise and call her blessed"; they were chosen next day for her memorial card. Cheerful, uncomplaining, thoughtful for the comfort and well-being of her guests to the last, Mrs Taylor, in her indomitable courage, kept the growing darkness at bay, and none saw that death stood beside her. Next day she took farewell of her remaining children as she rallied from a sudden collapse, then passed quietly into sleep and out of this world.

It was therefore a sadly stricken family that left the old home on 'the Rye' in May, and entered the pleasant, gracious house which stood on the plateau of Denmark Hill and formed part of Queen Anne's Gardens. The neighbourhood abounded in large and beautiful mulberry-trees; there was one in the Taylor's new garden, and opposite were the grounds of a small mansion, so that the outlook was over lawns and great, softly swaying trees—still a country view. And here Elsie took up the threads of her life again, striving through her own sense of irreparable loss to comfort and strengthen the younger ones of the family, and to be at hand as the close companion of her father. But in the New Year of 1888 there re-entered her life the man who was within a few months to become her husband. And he was to take her away to the Midlands to break new ground in the adventure of marriage and motherhood, and in a daily round of wider service than any she had yet known.

5

Courtship and Marriage

ELSIE TAYLOR first met her husband when she was a girl in her late teens. Her aunt, Caroline Barrow, had taken a cottage at Church Stretton for the summer, and invited Elsie Taylor and her sister Janet, still a schoolgirl, to spend their holidays with her. One evening, shortly after their arrival, a broad-shouldered, bearded man, already in early middle life, called upon Caroline Barrow, and was introduced to the Taylor sisters. He was George Cadbury, of Birmingham, who had already made his mark in the business world through the enterprise with which he and his brother, Richard, had built up the manufacture of cocoa and chocolates. He was staying at a near-by hotel with his wife, Mary Tylor, and his son Edward, then about five years old, and had come to enlist the help of Caroline Barrow in a Temperance meeting which he was organizing in the village of Church Stretton. Before he left, both Elsie and Janet found to their dismay that they had committed themselves to speak at this public gathering. After this first visit George Cadbury frequently joined Caroline Barrow and her two nieces in the excursions which the energetic aunt planned, and as they walked over the rolling hills together a friendship sprang up between Elsie and the business-man of vision, twenty years her senior.

"I, with other young people of the day, was longing to respond to the call of youth from prophets such as Carlyle, Ruskin, and Kingsley, to recognize our responsibility for the bad conditions under which thousands of our fellow citizens were living," says Elizabeth Cadbury, in a chapter of memories. "Matthew Arnold and others were preaching 'divine discontent.' I had then little practical experience of industrial life or conditions, or of housing defects and poverty, but had read a great deal. Here was a man who knew, and had a vision of a future with opportunities for all, good homes and amenities of life, and I listened eagerly to all he had to say. Besides this I was much flattered that a man much older than myself and with so much experience, should talk thus to a girl, immature though enthusiastic."

For the next ten years they met only occasionally when Elsie was staying with her Aunt Caroline Barrow at Birmingham, but she never forgot those talks, or the village of which George Cadbury dreamt, where the working people of Birmingham could live in pleasant, open surroundings, in well-built houses set in gardens, and with plenty of opportunity for outdoor exercise and recreation.

George Cadbury had the energy, the acumen, the self-discipline, of the nineteenth-century pioneer in industry. There was more than a little of the great adventurer in him, and an undeviating tenacity of purpose. He worked hard and steadily to acquire the wealth that came to him, but he wanted it primarily not for his self-gratification but for the power which it gave him to carry out his schemes for the good of others. That in itself may be a dangerous purpose, and George was not, perhaps, unaware of the danger. The human being remains curiously averse to having good done to him. But withal it remains true that to lift the burden of human misery and want was a first claim on George Cadbury's time and thought.

He too came of a long line of Quaker forebears, and was descended from a West Country family of yeomen and wool-combers. His grandfather, Richard Tapper Cadbury, known locally as "King Richard" or "King Dick" with his spruce and careful dress and a flower always sported in his buttonhole, was the first to settle in Birmingham, starting business in that city as a silk mercer in 1794. Both that grandfather, and his son John, the father of George Cadbury, were active members on the governing body of the town and much occupied in social work. John Cadbury started in business as a tea-dealer and coffee-roaster, and prepared "cocoa nibs" for a breakfast drink merely as a sideline. In 1861 he handed over this business, which was rapidly going downhill, to his two sons, Richard and George, aged twenty-five and twenty-two respectively. For the next few years they had a hard struggle to keep their heads above water, and success was only achieved by a rigid self-discipline, an extreme simplicity of life, and long hours of unremitting work. Their persistence, their courage, their vision of the possibilities, and their unshaken faith carried them through, and, with the manufacture of a purer cocoa than any yet to be found on the British market, their business began to prosper and grow.

In the year 1878 the two brothers took the momentous decision of removing their factory from its cramped quarters in the heart of the city to what was then the open countryside on the outskirts. A site was purchased on land which lay between the villages of Stirchley, King's Norton, and Selly Oak, some four miles from the city centre. The land, which was chiefly sloping meadow, ran down to the Bourn brook on the north and contained only one cottage. George Cadbury himself drew up the rough plans of the first factory, building started in January 1879, and in September the transfer of the business to its new home began.

Both brothers exercised a constant vigilance over the welfare of their workers; recreation grounds, heated cloakrooms where wet coats could dry during the day, separate dining-rooms where the workers could relax over a hot meal away from the noise of the machinery—these were unheard-of innovations for a factory of that period. In the early days at Bournville George Cadbury would interview all the new girls applying to be taken on; "we were like a family, often in personal touch with the masters," is the testimony of one who could remember those times,[1] and another speaks with affectionate amusement of the two brothers crawling under the tables to see if the water-pipes were really hot. The unceasing care of these two busy men for the comfort and well-being of those in their employ made a deep impression. Small wonder, in those days of bitter contest usual between factory owner and factory hand, that a crowd of applicants for service in the new factory was pressing eagerly around the gates on the day of its opening; the numbers employed jumped from 230 to over 300 immediately after the move.[2]

[1] See *The Firm of Cadbury, 1831–1931*, by Iolo A. Williams (1931), p. 101.
[2] By 1889 this figure had risen to nearly 1200, in 1899 it stood at 2685, and the area of factory buildings had trebled by the close of the nineteenth century. In 1930 the number of employees had stabilized at 8370; 4489 men, 3881 women. (See *The Firm of Cadbury, 1831–1931*, by Iolo A. Williams (1931), p. 101.) It is now some 10,000, besides those employed overseas.

In the year 1872, when his feet were firmly planted on the path of success, George Cadbury had married Mary Tylor, the daughter of a London Friend, Charles Tylor. Their first home was in Edgbaston, where the two eldest sons, Edward and George, were born, but in 1881 they moved to a large house, called Woodbrooke, surrounded by gardens and shrubberies, a short distance from the village of Selly Oak and from the new factory at Bournville. The three younger children of this marriage, Henry, Isabel, and Eleanor, were added to the family circle in the next few years after the move.

Her children remember Mary Tylor Cadbury as a quiet, retiring woman of scholarly habits and tastes and with a gift for languages. She gave much time and thought to the poor of her neighbourhood and her city, and it was under her régime that the practice arose of entertaining parties of children from the Sunday schools of Birmingham or of men and their wives from her husband's adult school class in the city, or the "poor mothers" of Stirchley, to parties held in a marquee on the lawns of Woodbrooke or in the meadows of the home farm near by. But the first Mrs Cadbury was not a committee woman, nor was she accustomed to take much part in the ordinary social life of her day. It was a quiet and happy family, following something of the customary Quaker retirement in the sanctuary of Woodbrooke, set among its great elms and beeches, its pleasant lawns, and brilliant beds of flowers. In 1887 that close-knit circle was suddenly and rudely broken by the death of Mary Cadbury, who left behind her five children, the eldest, Edward, a schoolboy of fourteen, the youngest, Eleanor, a mere baby.

George Cadbury, a man of forty-eight, as he emerged from the first darkness of his sorrow felt it essential to seek a new mother for his young family. He had known Mary Jane Taylor for some years and had cherished a great admiration for her, and he remembered the girl Elizabeth, his companion of the Shropshire hills, who had listened so eagerly to his plans for the development of Bournville and had responded to them with imaginative generosity and enthusiasm.

Early in the New Year of 1888 while on a visit to London he met John Taylor, and was invited to dine at Denmark Hill next day. That evening his friendship with Elsie was renewed, and rapidly deepened. By the beginning of February letters were passing almost daily between Woodbrooke and Denmark Hill; there were frequent meetings in London—gifts of flowers from the Woodbrooke conservatories, further eager discussions on social questions and the possibilities of effective service. On February 19 George Cadbury received the momentous letter in which Elsie accepted his formal proposal of marriage.

The news of the engagement, which was announced early in March, came as a surprise to Elsie's many friends and relatives. They had never heard her mention the name of George Cadbury —some did not know him even by repute; others, who knew of him, felt that he might be *nearly* good enough as a husband for their greatly loved Elsie. Her young brother John Augustine, writing from school, could hardly imagine her engaged, or the gap that would be left in the home circle by her going. But he was cheered by the thought that the wedding might be in term-time when he could have an unexpected holiday, and by the possibility of future supplies of chocolate.

The members of George Cadbury's family welcomed the newcomer with characteristic generosity, though the news of the engagement breaking upon them so soon after the death of Mary Cadbury undoubtedly came as something of a shock. But if some wished that a year might have been allowed to elapse before the announcement of a new wife and mother was made, the nearer relatives—John Cadbury, the father of George, his brother Richard, his sister Maria Fairfax, and his cousin Jessie, who had been keeping house for him since the death of his wife—all wrote rejoicing at the new happiness which the engagement had brought him.

Elizabeth Taylor herself inevitably faced the sudden plunge into a new life with greatly mixed feelings. No woman with her sense of responsibility could have taken such a step without grave misgivings, which, in a weaker nature, might have approached moments of panic. There was the difficult task of taking control of a family of five children not her own, in itself demanding an enduring courage; there was the disparity in age between the high-spirited woman of thirty and her future

D

husband, nearly twenty years her senior, sobered and tempered by the discipline of his greater experience of life. She looked to him with a somewhat shy admiration, and for a few weeks after her engagement he even had difficulty in getting her to use his Christian name, and she continued to address him in her daily letters as "My dearest Friend." And, in addition to the gulf of years, there was the burden of a greater wealth than she had ever dreamed of possessing—in itself a heavy responsibility to a young woman of her outlook and upbringing.

The surrender of the ties of her own close-knit family circle, where her presence was even more in demand since her mother's death, was a first great ordeal for Elsie to face. Then, too, all the work she had embarked upon through the years in London must be given up—the boys' clubs, the classes with girls and women and Sunday-school children—all the different groups to whom her gaiety and humour brought a new light and courage week by week; the place of leadership she had assumed among the young Friends in Essay and Portfolio Societies, who looked to her as the joyous companion in discussion groups or picnic parties and welcomed her daring introduction of music and drama into the sober gatherings of their elders—all this must go with her independence as she entered upon the state of marriage. But she was deeply and happily in love, and on the other side, heavily weighting the scales in George Cadbury's favour, was the chance of new and greater ventures in the different milieu of Birmingham, where already she had many friends. Best of all was the possibility of working with her husband in full partnership in the development of his plans for better housing conditions and social relationships.

So, in the crowded weeks that lay between February and her wedding in June, Elsie continued her usual round of activities, outwardly gay and courageous as ever if sometimes with a sinking heart as she faced the approaching farewells. She would steal away now and again for an afternoon at the Academy or on the river with George Cadbury, or a hurried visit to Dorking to spend a little time with her grandmother who had removed there some years before. Two or three week-ends were spent at a farm in the Malvern Hills; here George Cadbury brought his second son, George, that he might get to know his future step-mother in the course of walks and drives together, and the boy returned home quite captivated. Henry and Isabel, both small children, came on separate occasions for a few days to Denmark Hill, that Elsie might come to know them a little and not arrive as a complete stranger at Woodbrooke. The visits were a great success; she took them to the zoo, played with them among the mulberry-trees in the garden, or took them for drives in the carriage; Isabel forgot her shyness, and Henry was at home from the first. It was characteristic of Elsie that in planning for the visit of her little stepdaughter she remembered the agonies of shyness she had experienced in visiting an aunt when a small child, and suggested that Isabel ("Minnie") should be allowed to decide for herself whether or not she should come.

The weeks slipped by, and at last all was ready. On Tuesday, June 19, 1888, Elizabeth Taylor and George Cadbury were married in the Quaker Meeting House at Peckham Rye in the presence of a large gathering of Friends. Elsie noted in her diary that it was a good meeting for worship at which George Gillett spoke, and her father and her Uncle Tom prayed. Forty-four people, relatives and close friends, sat down to lunch in Denmark Hill afterwards, and then the bride and bridegroom left for Scotland, calling in at the Mothers' Meeting at Bunhill Fields on the way to Euston, to leave a wedding cake and to receive the congratulations and good wishes of the women. The first night of the honeymoon was spent at the Old Swan Inn in Stafford, and then came three weeks in Scotland with long days of sunshine and flaming sunsets, and the short, light nights of the northern zone. They landed at Portree, in Skye, by the light of a full moon; the tide was so low on arrival that the boat could not make the pier, and the passengers had to cross by a plank to the quay. Many of the women passengers could not face this ordeal and were landed in a boat, but it did not occur to Elsie Cadbury to be afraid, and she was the first to stride across. From Skye George Cadbury chartered a cutter, complete with skipper and crew, to sail to Stornoway.

"The boat was very jolly," writes Elsie to her sister Margaret, on June 27.

> We made most comfortable seats of shawls and rugs and old sails, for there was nothing whatever in the way of furniture; the sailors were Gaelic and most picturesque, romantic and interesting; we discussed the crofters' question. Picnicking was great fun, and the sailing was lovely *while it lasted*; but gradually the wind dropped, we went slower and slower, till at last the men had to confess we had barely gone a hundred yards in four hours. We then made up our minds to the inevitable in the shape of spending the night on board, and secondly, not going to Stornoway at all but across to Gairloch, for what little wind there was was dead against us. We got out into the tub that belonged to the boat, for exercise, though the men were dreadfully afraid we might drown as it was a rickety affair. They were very nervous; one nearly wept when George insisted on having a bathe in the morning!

So, with the beauty of a sunset and rising moon together, the afterglow not fading from the skies before dawn had broken, the newly married couple drifted through that night of splendour —"we were truly thankful to be becalmed."

The honeymoon ended with visits to Blairgowrie and Braemar, where they penetrated the grounds and the dairy of the castle without a pass, climbed the hills, and got caught in a snowstorm in the Cairngorms. They explored Aberdeen for an evening, and finally came to Edinburgh by way of the Tay Bridge and on their arrival spent their last night in climbing Arthur's Seat. On July 11 they returned home to Birmingham, filled with the peace and satisfaction of their closer knowledge of one another, and the new mistress of Woodbrooke records that they came back to "a lovely, flowery welcome, all perfect."

6

The Wife and Mother

WITH the arrival of their stepmother the life of the Cadbury children took on a swifter, more exciting, and more unsettling tempo than anything they had known in the past. One stepson remembered vividly in his seventies the innovations that she introduced; painted finger-plates on drawing-room doors, overhangings on mantlepieces, were swept away; the long sash windows that opened to a terrace and veranda on one side of the house were flung wide for all the winds of heaven to sweep through; flowers were banked in hall and sitting-rooms; and visitors came, thick and fast, to stay. Always there seemed to the children to be people coming and going—brothers and sisters, cousins and friends, of their stepmother. The house rang with voices and laughter, with the music of the piano, with the bustle of preparation for a dinner party, a reading circle, or a week-end gathering of the leaders of the Liberal party to discuss future policy.

There were many difficulties facing the new wife and mother. The early years of her marriage were shadowed by her father's failure on the Stock Exchange, which came after some months of a severe and alarming illness, when his partners, who were then non-Friends, gained increasing control of the business. The failure, involving many besides himself in loss and ruin, was a bitter draught indeed for his second daughter to stomach. But through the swelling tide of public criticism and censure she remained staunchly loyal to her father; not even from her husband would she brook any criticism of him. John Taylor left the country with his youngest daughter, Josephine, and spent the last years of his life in South Africa. He died in May 1894, in Cape Colony, after only a few hours' illness.

In her own household Elizabeth Cadbury was inevitably confronted with some troubled waters to negotiate in her new position. Her older stepchildren had many battles to fight with themselves, and at moments with her, before they could accept their invigorating young stepmother as a friend. Servants and children's nurses, who had known and loved the first Mrs Cadbury, were perforce critical of the newcomer and her different ways of handling the household. Elizabeth Cadbury faced it all with courage and good humour and an iron resolution to make a success of her marriage and to win the confidence of her little family circle.

The difficulties of her position as a stepmother must have been enhanced by the arrival in rapid succession of her own five older children, born between March 1889 and August 1894.[1] But she set herself, with consummate skill, to weld the two families into one from the outset, and succeeded so far that her own children did not realize that the older members were half-brothers and -sisters till they themselves were ten or eleven years of age, and a governess was resident in the house for over a year before, by a chance remark of a visitor, she too grasped the fact that some of her charges were the children of a former wife. Before the arrival of her first child, Laurence, Elizabeth Cadbury, making her preparations for the baby, found the time and the wisdom to dress a baby doll and prepare its layette for her little stepdaughter Eleanor, that she too might have something of her own to tend and care for when her stepmother was necessarily absorbed with the new arrival. The mother's attitude was such that instead of jealousy there appears to have been spontaneous rejoicing as the birth of each baby was made known to the other children. In 1894, when Marion (or Mollie, as she was always called) was born, a governess in charge of six of the older children, who had been sent to Boulogne, wrote to Elizabeth Cadbury, "The little girls are wildly excited; when I asked them to guess the news Eleanor did so at second try. The children's remarks are all most comic; Isabel wishes that 'when you were at it you had bought four.'" With such a wish, we can gather that Elizabeth had succeeded reasonably well in her first task of holding the growing family together.

[1] Laurence John (1889), George Norman (1890), Elsie Dorothea (1892), Egbert (1893), Marion Janet (1894).

Woodbrooke was becoming somewhat cramped to meet the needs of the expanding household, so in the year 1894 George Cadbury purchased a house in Northfield, known as the Manor House, which stood on the opposite side of the Bristol road from Woodbrooke, and was a mile or so farther from Birmingham. It was built on the site of a farm established about 1750; various additions to the original homestead had been made by subsequent occupiers in the course of the nineteenth century, and further alterations and extensions were put in hand by the Cadburys on the completion of the purchase. "The main front rooms are part of the old building," wrote Elizabeth in 1943; "the Library, the room we mostly live in, was two rooms made into one. We enlarged the room on the left-hand side of the entrance, pushed the hall back and made a new staircase, necessitating a new kitchen and other service departments. The attic floor we converted into several good bedrooms. So all that accounts for the general aspect of the house now."

Only a week before the birth of Mollie Elizabeth was climbing up ladders to inspect the work and make sure that it was to her satisfaction. A month after the birth she travelled out to Boulogne with the baby, and spent some weeks there with her older children, and the family then returned together to the house at Northfield, which was to be the home of Elizabeth Cadbury for the rest of her life. To organize the move and carry it through smoothly with a two-months-old baby, a second child of just over a year, and three others, aged two, four, and five respectively, was in itself no mean feat!

The large, rambling house, with its spacious rooms and great bay windows through which the sunlight flooded, is the home that her children remember. A long, tree-lined avenue, branching into two a little below the house, ran for some quarter of a mile from the Bristol road. It crossed a noisy brook, with miniature waterfalls, flowing out from a large pond; stretches of lawn and parkland sloped down to the water from the front of the house, and everywhere great trees—beeches, oaks, and elms—spread the delicate tracery of their bare branches or the richness of their summer foliage. A single towering Wellingtonia thrust its spire upwards from a stretch of lawn before the front door. Later a flagged terrace and a loggia were added where meals were taken out of doors from early spring to late autumn.

Far away, at the head of the vegetable and flower gardens, stood a cottage which was used as an isolation ward when one or other of the children fell ill with an infectious disease. It was occupied throughout the greater part of the childhood of the Cadburys by Mr and Mrs Pitt, the gardener and his wife, and when the cottage was called into use as an isolation hospital Mrs Pitt did the housekeeping for the sick child and its nurse.

A large staff was maintained to run the house and gardens, the stables, the nursery, and the schoolroom—twenty people or more in those far-off, leisured days. Many of them were people of great character whose personalities made an indelible impression on the Cadbury children. Barrett, the estate carpenter, was the hero of the little boys, teaching them (and subsequently their sons) to handle their first tools in the carpenter's and engineering shops which their parents had provided in the outbuildings of the Manor. He had sailed all round the world as a ship's carpenter, and came to the Manor first to work on the alterations of the house, remaining in the service of the Cadbury's until his death shortly before the Second World War. There were the coachmen, Wheeler and Bradley, the latter with three sons acting as travellers for the Cadbury firm at one time, whose boast it was that he would never shoot a rabbit until he could get two with one shot. Wheeler graduated to the position of chauffeur in the early days of motoring and shared many adventures with Elizabeth Cadbury in those days of frequent breakdowns, which often involved her in a long and weary tramp homeward through rain or snow. There was Oakes, the completely illiterate but very efficient farm bailiff, and Hughes, the second gardener, who would appear every Christmas Eve to sing long folk-songs from his native Oxfordshire for the children's delectation. He muttered wrathfully about the rule of "petticoat government" when Elizabeth introduced a lady head-gardener, but learned to work in harmony with her eventually.

But the central figure of the early household at the Manor was Jeanne Leroy, who was introduced as a protégée of George Cadbury's sister, Maria Fairfax, and came from Boulogne

(where that sister lived) to act as the children's nurse when
Mollie was two years old. She stayed for fifty years and died
at the Manor only three years before her greatly loved employer.
As the children grew beyond her care, and passed into the charge
of governesses or went away to school, Jeanne remained in close
personal attendance on Elizabeth, seeing to all things within the
household for which the busy mother had no time. Upright,
calm, imperturbable whatever crisis might arise, she was a
tower of strength to the whole family, the loved and practical
friend who understood and met the manifold needs of childhood
and youth.

When their family had grown up, and many of its members
had already scattered to different parts of the British Isles in
homes of their own, George and Elizabeth, taking Jeanne with
them, went for a holiday to France and bought her a little
boarding-house in her native land to provide a fresh life and
interest for her. They left her established happily, as they thought,
and continued their holiday farther afield. When they reached
Boulogne a few weeks later on their way home there was
Jeanne awaiting them. She could not leave them, she said,
for she missed them so, and all the coming and going of
their children. And so, to every one's delight, she returned
to Birmingham, and nothing was ever again said about her
leaving.

The pace at which Elizabeth lived, each day filled with its
round of committees and public meetings, wore out many a
companion and secretary. But those who could adjust themselves to the tempo of life and stay the course were unfailingly
devoted to her. She never suffered fools gladly; blessed with
excellent health and an iron constitution, she was apt to be
impatient of the frailty of those not so richly endowed. But to
all who won her regard and friendship, whether they were in
her employ or no, she remained throughout life utterly loyal in
her affections. She had the gift of sharing her interests with those
who worked for her, kindling in them the fires of her own
enthusiasm, so that they embarked together as colleagues on
her many ventures. Miss Downes, who came as governess to the
older children, and remained after they had gone to school as

the secretary of Elizabeth Cadbury, not only aided her untiringly in her Adult School, Y.W.C.A., and girls' club work,
but eventually became so engrossed in these concerns that she
left Mrs Cadbury after more than twenty years of service to
devote herself wholly to an administrative post in the Y.W.C.A.
"I never worked for anyone so devoid of pettiness," was the
testimony, after Elizabeth's death, of her last personal secretary.
"Mrs Cadbury never bore a grudge, nor did she remember a
mistake for more than a few minutes."

How much those valiant helpers who could meet her demands
became a part of the family circle is suggested by the fact that
Elizabeth Cadbury's second stepson, George, married in 1902
Edith Caroline Woodall, who had come for a time to teach
the younger children, and her brother, Wilfrid, while on holiday
in England in 1904 and staying at the Manor House, fell in love
with, and married, her secretary, a young American woman
called Elizabeth Knox Taylor. It was to the latter that the child
Dorothea remarked one day, "Barrett always talks of the man
who helps him as his mate and Laurence calls Norman 'mate.'
Now, I have often wondered what you are to Mother, and I
suppose you are a mate-ess." The child's suggestion reveals the
happy relationship that existed between Mrs Cadbury and her
personal assistants.

Remembering the days of her own childhood, Elizabeth
gave to her children and stepchildren a very full measure of
freedom. There was always an element of surprise in their
mother's dealings with them. She returned home one evening
to find that Dorothea and Mollie had been sent to bed in disgrace
for climbing on the roof of the Manor. Elizabeth's reaction was
immediate—"Excellent, it will teach them to keep their heads
and give them a sense of balance. Get them up again at once."
Or there would be a sudden decision to go to London for a few
days of sightseeing, shopping, and theatres, the word being given
at the children's supper-time, and their suitcases being packed
forthwith that they might get off by the early train from
Birmingham.

Elizabeth herself, in one of her public addresses, has left on
record the attempt to find a happy medium between the strict

discipline which governed Victorian childhood and the demand
for unbridled self-expression that followed. Important as it was,
she said, to read some of the many treatises on psychology and
hygiene, even more important was it for parents to try to understand the minds and to study the varying dispositions of their
children.

The responsibility of the parent does not end with the choice of a
good school; sympathetic participation in games and pursuits or
care of physical health . . . it is the home 'atmosphere' (over-
worked but inevitable word) that is one of the most important and
potent factors in determining whether a child shall be a help or a
hindrance in the world to-day.

In a house where the conversation and general tendency are in
the direction of self-indulgence, where wealth and luxury are the
ultimate goal, where motor-cars, dances and amusements are
paramount considerations, even if they succeed in shielding their
children from grosser and less legitimate indulgences, parents
cannot be said to have grasped the extent of their responsibilities.
Again, in a home where the inequalities of opportunity, position
and wealth are disregarded, where the just demand of the industrial
workers for decent conditions, for adequate wages, for respectable
homes, for the amenities of life are ignored, where 'foreigners,'
who for the time being happen to be classed as 'enemies,' are therefore 'knaves, liars, and murderers,' and where most other 'foreigners,'
whoever they may be, are inferior to the superior British race, in
all such homes parents are failing to do their duty as patriots and as
householders in the Kingdom of God. . . .

National and international problems alike are calling to parents
at all points of the compass to face their responsibilities, and the
parent who neglects to train his children in the right attitude to all
such questions is foolish, short-sighted, and will soon be a back
number.

With patience and imagination, with care and affection,
Elizabeth built up an enduring friendship with her children and
stepchildren, and gave to each the sense that their relationship
with her was particular and unique. She threw herself whole-
heartedly into plans for their amusement and interest. Every
Christmas a party was given for the staff and their families, at
which the Cadbury children would act plays, coached by their

mother; in diverse ways she drew the whole household together as a living community in which each member had his significant part to play, his contribution to give.

In her manifold self-imposed tasks Elizabeth must perforce leave the younger children to the care of nurses and governesses for the greater part of the day. But she always tried to hurry home to spend the last hours before bedtime with them. On Sunday evenings she would gather them round the organ, which George Cadbury had had built for her in the "oak room," to sing songs and hymns, and then would read aloud to them from the English poets, of whom Tennyson and Browning were among her favourites, as they grew old enough to appreciate at least the music of words and rhythm.

School holidays were always sacrosanct, when the parents devoted themselves to the children. A house would be taken on the Yorkshire Moors or the East Coast, on a Scottish loch or in Cornwall, and the little crowd would set forth, from the last baby in arms to the older stepsons and daughters in their 'teens, with nurses and maids accompanying them, travelling to their destination in a reserved saloon coach. Part of the joy of the journey was in visiting at intervals the pony in his loose-box, who would be brought along too, with a trap, to drive the children about the countryside. Busy up to the last moment, Elizabeth would join the party just as the train was about to move, dashing up the platform as the guard's whistle blew. "My recreation begins," she tells us, "the moment when I drop, after an agitating race with time, into a comfortable railway carriage, and having counted my family to see that none is missing, prepare to enjoy a delicious sense of leisure. The father of the family, who likes to arrive at the station thirty minutes before the indicated hour of departure, does not appreciate the keen pleasure experienced by my methods!"

In 1898 Elizabeth and George, leaving the three youngest children behind, ventured on a holiday abroad with six of the older ones. Most of the time was spent in travel; the party visited Lucerne, Wengen, Grindelwald, Mürren, and Berne, covering a great deal of ground by a horse-drawn 'diligence.' "A glorious holiday," notes the indefatigable mother, still untired after trailing around two boys aged eight and nine years, and two girls of thirteen and fourteen, in addition to two youths in their late 'teens and early twenties.

Malvern was always a favourite resort for the Easter break; it had long been a greatly loved retreat of George Cadbury's. For many years the family stayed at the same farm, where they knew the proprietors well, but in 1897, in conjunction with Richard Cadbury and his family, they purchased a house on the Malvern Hills, called Wind's Point. This had once been a home of the Swedish singer Jenny Lind, and contained many of her relics.

At first the two families and their friends would occupy the house in different months; but, on the death of his brother, George took over the whole responsibility for this second and very lovely home, which stood on a spur of the hills close by the British Camp, a great hill fortress of the early Iron Age.

Seldom can a house have been so abundantly and generously used as a place of quiet retreat—for children convalescing from illness, for old people to snatch a little hard-earned rest, for gatherings of friends, children, grandchildren, and great-grand-children, or for the celebration of some festival in the families of close friends and relatives. The Cadbury children came here each Easter, leaving the train at Malvern Wells to drive or cycle the last few miles, jumping from the carriage or dismounting from their bicycles to trudge up the long hill on foot, with the scent of the spring countryside about them and the days of holiday gleaming ahead. At first the house was lighted by oil lamps and candles, but riotous games were played in its rooms in the spring or winter evenings; Elizabeth Cadbury looked on unperturbed, or joined in the less tempestuous romps, apparently oblivious to the danger of oil lamps which might come crashing to the floor as a whirlwind chase swept past them.

In 1927 Sir Oliver and Lady Lodge, who were very close friends of Elizabeth, celebrated their Golden Wedding here; to this place of peace and quietude came Sir Henry Campbell-Bannerman after the death of his wife, and in long talks with his host found some measure of healing in his sorrow. Canon and

Mrs Barnett, two other great friends of the family, would find weeks of refreshment here from the throb and pain of life in the East End. Sir George Newman, at one time Chief Medical Officer of the Board of Education, sought rest here from his medical and administrative labours; Dean Inge, Bernard Shaw, Mr and Mrs Bramwell Booth, were among the multitude of guests whom the house welcomed.

In the early years of this century George and Elizabeth Cadbury rented for several seasons the villa of Monte Verde at Bordighera. It then became the custom for the parents and their younger children to spend several weeks here in the spring of each year, and to entertain various friends passing to and from Italy. The youngest of Dame Elizabeth's children, Ursula, born in 1906, nearly twelve years after the rest, passed a great deal of time here in her early years, and her daughter, Dorothea (Dollie), celebrated her twenty-first birthday at Bordighera. The villages around, nestling among the rocks, provided countless opportunities for exploration; the local peasants became firm friends of the family, and the wealth of spring flowers—mimosa, anemones, freesia, and rosemary—were in themselves a refreshment to mind and spirit.

But housekeeping in a foreign tongue presented certain difficulties and unforeseen results. After wrestling with her Italian chef in the endeavour to initiate him into the mysteries of making a Malvern pudding, with jam, sponge-cakes, and custard, the feelings of the mother can be imagined when she found that the dish set before her on the table contained slices of thick, rich ham instead of jam.

George Cadbury had been brought up in the narrower Puritan tradition of an earlier generation of Quakers. It was Elizabeth who opened to him the delights of music and poetry, and later of the theatre. She brought him a new zest for life, getting him to learn golf, a game which he came greatly to enjoy; in the long summer evenings when he returned from his crowded day at Bournville she would tempt him on to the tennis court to find fresh vigour in the battle across the net with herself and the older children as partners and opponents.

As the children, one by one, passed from the sunny schoolroom at the Manor to their various preparatory and public schools,[1] Elizabeth's loving and unobtrusive care followed them into the new chapter of life that was opening. Every week, whatever the pressure of events, each child away at school or college received a letter from her, detailing the news of home and of other members of the family, giving wise counsel at any moment of need. One of her stepchildren stated to the writer that those weekly letters to him at school were among the gifts of life which he valued most; they were a crucial factor in determining his attitude and his outlook on the world.

While the boys were at Leighton Park, London Yearly Meeting, the annual gathering of the Society of Friends, became a festive occasion for the young Cadburys. For the schoolboys came up at the week-end, put in an appearance at one or other of the Yearly Meeting sessions, and then were carried off by their mother on a round of sight-seeing; the Academy, the White City, Earl's Court, a trip up the river, an afternoon at Maskelyne and Cook's, or an evening at the theatre. Naturally, Yearly Meeting was an occasion to anticipate eagerly and look back upon with pleasure.

Elizabeth's unerring knowledge of the children under her care could withstand disappointments; her faith in them remained unshaken by apparent failure to realize and make good

[1] The eldest son, Edward, had been sent to the Friends' School known as Oliver's Mount in Scarborough before his father's second marriage. With his growing family George Cadbury became very interested in, and in part responsible for, the project of founding a Quaker school, run on public-school lines, at Reading. Leighton Park was opened in 1890, and here George, Henry, Laurence, Norman, and Egbert were all sent in turn, after a period at various preparatory schools.

The girls, as they reached the age for boarding school, were sent to various foundations; Isabel to Southwold and later to the Mount School at York, Eleanor to St Andrews, in Scotland, where her own daughters were later pupils, Dorothea and Mollie, after a time at the Girls' High School in Edgbaston, to St James's, at West Malvern. Ursula was considered too delicate to be sent away, and was educated at home. A governess, Miss Stuart, trained in P.N.E.U. methods, was engaged for her. She was teaching the little daughter of the author Archibald Marshall at the time of her appointment, and Betty Marshall came to the Manor with her to share Ursula's lessons. Throughout her childhood she lived there for months at a time, becoming almost a sixth daughter, and remaining one of the closest friends of Ursula.

their hidden capacities. Her stepson Henry Tylor Cadbury[1] was a frail and delicate child when she entered his world, and from the first she took him as her special charge. Throughout his youth the predominant influence was his stepmother's; her affection and her belief in him were the factors that strengthened his resolve, that put the necessary iron into his sensitive and diffident nature. As a schoolboy at Leighton Park, Henry Cadbury described himself as hopelessly dull and backward; when he left he was still in one of the lowest forms and the oldest boy in that class. His father and older brothers, in despair of his making any success of business or profession, suggested that he should take up social work, as, in a different section of society, the son who apparently lacked ability was often allotted to the Church! But Elizabeth Cadbury, with steadfast conviction that there were undeveloped powers of a high order in this slowly maturing son, insisted that he should be sent to Cambridge. There his latent capacities blossomed, and he had a successful academic career. "But I owe it entirely to my mother that I had that opportunity," he said.

He recalled also, with gratitude, that during this unsatisfactory period of his life, when he returned home for the holidays one summer as a boy of about fifteen, feeling keenly his position as a disappointment in an able family, Elizabeth at once realized the situation and his need. She was temporarily without a secretary and asked the baffled, silent schoolboy if he would be willing to act in that capacity during his vacation. He leapt at the suggestion, and morning after morning would sit with his stepmother, going through her voluminous correspondence, noting the sort of reply she wanted sent in each case, and spending the next hours writing out a dozen letters or so by hand for her signature. The work and the trust imposed in him began to build up his shaken self-confidence; "It made me feel I was wanted," he said. But it needed a clever woman, with an unusual insight into the needs of a difficult adolescent, to hit on that particular solution—perhaps one of the few tasks that could have restored his self-respect. How amply his stepmother's faith in him was justified the coming years were to show, when, as managing

[1] Henry Tylor Cadbury died on September 25, 1952, in his seventieth year.

director of the *Daily News*, Henry Cadbury brought that paper out of a period of financial difficulty and decline into the ranks of the big London dailies with one of the largest circulations in the country.

None of the children ever wanted to go away to spend a holiday with their school friends; for them home was the place of radiant happiness and fun, to which they brought their school companions for a share in its joys. Even after marriage, the first place of choice for a holiday was still the Manor with its warm and loving welcome for every child, for each son and daughter-in-law, for grandchildren and great-grandchildren. The centre of that home, holding the family together in bonds of affection and mutual confidence that survived the strains of adolescence and adult life, was the mother, Elizabeth Cadbury. Behind all the outward activities, in which she stood beside her husband, working steadily and tirelessly, behind all the new ventures in service which she pursued on her own initiative, there remained always the wife and mother, the gracious hostess, the skilful ruler of the home with all its diverse personalities to consider and handle. In that more restricted, intimate field perhaps Elizabeth did some of her greatest work.

7

The First Years of Service in Birmingham (1888-1900)

ALTHOUGH she was a widely travelled woman, the greater part of Elizabeth's life was passed in the city of Birmingham to which she came as a bride. If there was little outwardly attractive in that busy industrial centre, which had grown haphazard from a country village throughout the past two centuries, there was a vigorous and challenging local life with a long tradition of independent and radical thought behind it. Dr Joseph Priestley, "the father of modern chemistry," Matthew Boulton and James Watt, whose inventions had transformed the country's industry, John Baskerville, the great printer—these were among the shades that hovered about the roads of Edgbaston, the districts of Fairhill and Soho. The Lunar Society,[1] founded in 1766 for purposes of philosophical and scientific discussion, whose membership included some of the most brilliant men of the age, had lent a sparkling lustre to the grimy, throbbing, striving town that was already thrusting out into the Warwickshire countryside.

From the latter years of the eighteenth century an active role in the business and social life of Birmingham had been played by Unitarians and Quakers, who had come in some numbers to make their homes in the town.[2] The Unitarian families of

[1] So-called because it met on nights when the moon was full, that the members might return to their homes along unlit roads and streets in greater safety when the meetings closed at eight o'clock. Besides the men mentioned above, Erasmus Darwin, grandfather of Charles, Josiah Wedgwood the great potter, and Sir Josiah Banks, president of the Royal Society, were members of the group.

[2] It has been estimated that in 1700 there was one member of the Society of Friends to every sixty inhabitants of Birmingham. (Charles Dickinson Sturge: *Old Families, Birmingham Meeting*. MS. in Bevan-Naish Library, Birmingham, 1892.)

Chamberlain, Kenrick, Martineau, and Nettlefold, the Quaker families of Lloyd, Sturge, Baker, and Cadbury, had opened a record of steady, patient service to their community which is still in the course of being written. They offered that service as part of a family tradition, not merely as individuals, and thereby gave to the civic life of Birmingham a basis of personal concern, a sense of continuity and of corporate responsibility, which was rare in the raw industrial towns of the nineteenth century.

From 1873 to 1876, in the decade before Elizabeth arrived in her new home, Joseph Chamberlain, the vigorous Unitarian Mayor, had launched and carried through his campaign for radical municipal reform and his plans for rebuilding the centre of the city, and had left it with the proud claim to be "the best governed city in the world." Rookeries of slums had been swept away; the broad thoroughfare of Corporation Street, flanked with its solid blocks of shops and offices, had been driven through them; and behind that façade some forty acres were allotted as a housing estate for the workers. Gas and water supplies were purchased by the Corporation and were bringing in a handsome return to the community; the town was alight with the spirit of adventure, the desire to experiment, the eagerness to discuss and to test new ideas. It was a climate particularly suited to the disposition of Elizabeth Cadbury.

The impulse behind the local initiative and the development of Birmingham's social gospel was and remained a religious one. Nonconformist preachers and teachers, who had played a leading part in rousing the citizens to action, believed firmly that they were working as surely for the Kingdom of God when they fought a municipal election as when they entered the pulpit on Sundays. The expression of that religious motive found an outlet in many ways in the course of the town's history. It was a Quaker citizen of Birmingham, Joseph Sturge, who founded in 1841 the Complete Suffrage Union, working to achieve universal manhood suffrage and provide a platform on which reformers of every party, including the dreaded Chartists, could unite and come to understand one another. It was in Birmingham also that the same Joseph Sturge, aided by the Quaker printer William

White, who served as one of Joseph Chamberlain's lieutenants in his plans of reconstruction, set on foot a modernized form of the Adult School Movement. A conference of teachers drawn from all the existing Friends' Adult Schools was held in Birmingham in 1847, and as an outcome of that meeting the Friends' First Day School Association was born. For the next three-quarters of a century it was to be the principal field of activity through which the Society sought to reach the working classes of the country.

George Cadbury, in 1859, had been drawn into the work of the Adult School which Joseph Sturge had opened at Severn Street. From 1863 he was given charge of a class of men, Class XIV, with which his connexion remained unbroken for fifty years. Every Sunday morning in all weathers it was his practice to ride into Severn Street on horseback[1] to hold his class and to share in the breakfast provided for the teachers before the Adult School opened at 7.30 A.M. On the first Sunday morning after her return from her honeymoon Elizabeth accompanied her husband to meet his men and their wives, who had come on this occasion to greet her. The women urged her to organize a similar school which they could attend, and within a few months this was accomplished. Thereafter, until her death, Elizabeth maintained contact with this Women's Adult School, which met at Severn Street on Monday afternoons, welcoming daughters and grand-daughters of the earlier members. It was her first venture into public service in Birmingham, and the school always held a very particular place in her affections and allegiance. Later another school was opened at Northfield, to which also she gave untiring weekly service. The classes were centred on the Bible lesson, where the early teaching of her own father in Peckham bore fruit. But she was quick to see the possibility of the Adult School as a training-ground in thought, an opportunity for wider education in the days when there were few agencies to help the adult man or woman to increase his range of knowledge and understanding. She had the gift of opening fresh horizons of thought, a new spaciousness of vision, by a

[1] A bicycle was later substituted for the horse, which was an advantage "because it gave no trouble at either end of the journey."

few vivid sentences, as she shared with her women the experiences of her own travels abroad, discussed with them some current problem of the day or some book recently read which had raised new questions in her mind. It was all linked skilfully with the study of the Bible, showing how the experience of prophet and psalmist or of the writers of the gospels had light to throw upon questions of the hour. The afternoons passed all too quickly, and the women returned to their homes and the often monotonous routine of the housewife and mother with some new, big idea to ponder, some scene of a sunset over the snows of the Jungfrau, or the wine-dark shadows chasing across the Mediterranean, to bring an unfamiliar beauty flashing into a busy moment of dusting or cooking.

Closely allied with the Adult Schools were a number of 'fellowship meetings' which had been started to provide a simple evening service for those to whom the orthodox church or chapel held little appeal. Several of these were held weekly in the growing suburbs of Birmingham; Elizabeth in her first days at Woodbrooke attended one at Selly Oak, and thereafter, at least once a month, she was present at one or other of these gatherings in Bournville, Selly Oak, or Stirchley, sometimes giving the address, sometimes accompanying the hymns or leading the singing. These 'fellowships' were largely the outcome of the Quaker Meeting for Worship which Richard and George Cadbury had started in 1883 by inviting the few Friends who lived in the neighbourhood to meet with them Sunday by Sunday in a small room at the Bournville factory. On the far side of the railway which ran from the city to Bournville lay the populous district of Stirchley, which, although it was then surrounded by the open country, contained a large proportion of slum dwellers. There was no place of recreation or refreshment for these people, save the public-house, and the needs of Stirchley weighed much upon the minds of the two brothers. They therefore decided to build a roomy institute on the main street of the village as a social and educational centre, and this was opened in 1892. The building quickly became the headquarters of a number of activities, including a flourishing Adult School, a children's Sunday school, temperance and savings societies, and allied causes. A coffee-room, classrooms, and a meeting house to accommodate 500 people were included in the Institute; the Meeting for Worship at Bournville was transferred here, and gained a large accession of attenders.[1]

Similar institutes on the lines of Stirchley were built at North-field and Selly Oak in 1892 and 1893, both largely financed by the Cadbury brothers, and in both Quaker Meetings for Worship were held on Sunday mornings, Sunday schools for the children of the neighbourhood in the afternoon, and crowded meetings of the "Christian fellowship" in the evenings. All these activities and meetings for worship traced their origin to the gathering of Friends called together at Bournville by Richard and George Cadbury. In all of them Elizabeth Cadbury maintained a living and practical interest, and either she herself or one of her sons and daughters as they grew up would be present regularly on Sunday evenings to take or to assist the service.

It was in the Midlands also that the first tentative steps towards a closer fellowship between the Nonconformist churches were taken, and Birmingham was soon in the forefront of this movement. Councils representative of the various denominations were formed in half a dozen towns between 1881 and 1890, a development which George Cadbury watched with keen interest. He warmly welcomed the suggestion for the formation of a Free Church Council in Birmingham which came from the Wesleyan Methodists, and proposed that as a first step a census of attendance at places of worship should be carried out. This was done in Birmingham and its suburbs on Sunday, November 27, 1892. The inquiry showed that in the 426 available churches, chapels, and mission halls not much more than half the seating accommodation was occupied, and even so the actual provision for public worship in the city was adequate for only 27 per cent. of the total population.[2] As a result, George Cadbury called a

---

[1] It was still known as the "Bournville Meeting," and was first recognized as a Preparative, in distinction from an Allowed, Meeting in January 1891. Elizabeth Cadbury became the first Preparative Meeting Clerk, with her stepson Edward as Assistant Clerk, a happy association in office which continued for some years.

[2] The Life of George Cadbury, by A. G. Gardiner (Cassell and Co., Ltd.), p. 164 ff.

conference early in 1893, with the approval of various Free Church leaders, which was attended by nearly 300 ministers and representatives of the dissenting churches. Birmingham was mapped out into 161 areas, in which each chapel was allotted its particular district or 'parish,' and undertook a house-to-house visitation. In November 1893, on the basis of this first co-operative effort, the Birmingham Free Church Council was inaugurated at a public meeting, with George Cadbury in the chair. He was elected the first president of the Birmingham Council, and held that office till 1898.

In the meantime, the extension of the movement on national lines had been attempted. Two national congresses of the Free Churches were held at Manchester and Leeds in 1892 and 1894 respectively, but though a council of elected representatives from all these churches was formed, the venture was weak and in danger of lapsing in its infancy. The powerful Birmingham federation turned the scale. The Congress was invited to meet in that city in 1895, and it was at the Birmingham Conference that the National Free Church Council was firmly established. Richard and George Cadbury undertook to finance the new body for the first five years of its existence, and George continued to make his contribution right up to the time of his own passing.

Elizabeth followed these events, step by step, with the most watchful interest. She met and talked with the Free Church leaders, with such men as Dr John Clifford, the great Baptist preacher and social reformer, Dr R. W. Dale, who had made famous the pulpit of Carr's Lane Chapel in Birmingham and was a leader in the city's programme of social reform, the Rev. Hugh Price Hughes, who revolutionized the Methodist Church of his day, and many others. Despite the growing secularism and materialism of the age, she was convinced that men and women of all classes were searching eagerly for truth—for the reality of the things that endure. The responsibility for aiding men in that difficult and even perilous quest rested, she believed, upon all practising Christians. In face of that need, doctrinal differences were of little account to her. A matter of the first importance was the mobilization of the forces of the spirit

against the evils rampant in her world—the exploitation of man
by man, the poverty of the workers, the unemployed, the aged;
the ignorance and lust for power that bred the seeds of class and
national war.

Many Friends looked askance at the movement and held aloof
from it, though some joined whole-heartedly in the effort to
find a new unity within the Protestant communion. The question
is one upon which they still hold divided opinions. But Elizabeth
Cadbury believed firmly that the battle for religious liberty in
which all the dissenters had shared, and the suffering of their
early members for the faith that was in them, had forged a bond
of enduring texture. If the new challenge offered to religion
by the changing concepts of society and of justice was to be
met, it might certainly be argued, as she did, that a united witness
on the part of the Churches to the basic principles of Christianity
was the one hope of doing so effectively. The dissenters themselves, under the leadership of such men as Hugh Price Hughes,
were shifting their emphasis from the claims of the individual
conscience with its independent choice and judgment, to the
corporate testimony of the group or church, and the need for
efficient organization. In their effort to be positive and constructive, to find an answer to the social challenge of the day,
Hugh Price Hughes urged upon his fellow Nonconformists
that "The unit of this movement is not the individual Christian
but the church." It was a new note unheard before in the history
of Nonconformity. But both George and Elizabeth Cadbury
were quick to respond to it.

If Birmingham itself was a stirring place in which to live, the
closing decades of the nineteenth century were equally an
exciting period for a woman to come to the full maturity of her
middle years. The old customary routines were being challenged,
were being swept away, and women were themselves making
demands that shook to its foundations many a solid, conservative
home. The reforms of the seventies, and particularly of Glad-
stone's first administration, had laid the foundations of the new
kind of state demanded by changing conditions. An expanding
Civil Service was recruited not by patronage but by competitive
examination; a growing volume of health legislation was devolved

upon the bodies responsible for local affairs, but was controlled by a strong central authority; a system of universal education was opened to the people by the foundation of State elementary schools in 1870, providing for a better educated electorate of the expanded franchise; Army reforms were taken in hand, and the purchase of commissions was abolished; the older universities were opened on approximately equal terms to Nonconformist and Roman Catholics as well as to churchmen; new social claims on the State were being voiced by a rising Labour movement.

In the year of Elizabeth's marriage the Act had been passed which took the conduct of local affairs out of the hands of the Justices of the Peace, whose authority had held unquestioned sway since the days of the first Elizabeth, and passed them over to elective county councils—a swing from aristocratic to demo-cratic government in the counties which was revolutionary. And it was in the eighties too that the militant Trade Unionism, whose prophets were John Burns and Tom Mann, first made its voice heard, demanding new rights and responsibilities for the working man. In the general election of 1892 eight candidates were nominated as direct representatives of Labour, independent of either of the existing parties, and two were returned to Parliament. In 1883, nine years previously, the Fabian Society had been founded, with its doctrine of municipal socialism and State control, and its campaign of gradualism, which was to permeate society with the collectivist ideal as opposed to the sturdy individualism of the Liberal and Radical tradition. There was indeed a sense that the people of England were on the move, if none quite knew whither.

George and Elizabeth were sympathetic to the Trade Unions as the guardians of the workers' rights, and George had en-couraged the formation of a Union at Bournville as a matter of example. But both realized that something more far-reaching was needed if the condition of the people was to become a living issue in local politics. The birth of a new political party, the Labour Party, was therefore welcomed by them, and they were on terms of friendship with many of its leaders, particularly Keir Hardie, Ramsay MacDonald, and John Burns. The latter arrived at the Manor first as an unexpected guest in 1896, and quickly won the regard of his hostess. But to Elizabeth, as to her husband, her point of contact with the workers' movement lay in the desire to see justice done, to strive ceaselessly for such immediate practical ends as the provision of decent houses and working conditions and a liberal system of education, and to achieve some measure of security for the old and the sick. Neither was interested in doctrinaire teachings—Socialist, Communist, or Conservative; both would repudiate the theory of inevitable class warfare. Elizabeth's political faith was coloured by the thought of the Christian Socialists, whose works she had read as a young woman; its basis, like theirs, was a religious one. This is made clear in an address which she gave in the early years of the twentieth century, in which she states:

> The service of Christ himself to the poor and needy is a motive more likely to be permanently efficient in stimulating men and women to genuine social service than a mere diffused goodwill towards their less fortunate fellows, or than a desire that their city, or nation may bear a good name, or may be more go-ahead than others in social efficiency. We need something that will arouse a true altruism—something that will energize the wills of men and women, consistently and over long periods of time, to sacrifice their time, their money, and their ease in the service of those who can never repay them, and may very probably requite them with ingratitude.
>
> We need something that will create, not a patronizing, fashionable craze for 'slumming,' not a mere organization of philanthropic endeavour, but a genuine spirit of brotherhood, which will enable those more fortunately placed to set themselves without any feeling of superiority (which would poison everything) on the same plane as those they are trying to serve. In my own belief nothing less than a religious motive can supply this needed spirit of the true social service.

An immediate and great opportunity was opened to Elizabeth in the first years of her marriage, with the planning of the village of Bournville for housing the workers of the city. In 1888 this was still only a dream in the mind of George Cadbury, but within four years of her wedding-day Elizabeth saw the work really beginning. Morning by morning she would walk through the fields from her home to the factory with her husband as he set off for his day's work, discussing with him the development of the village—where the roads should run and the shopping centre should lie, what type of house and cottage should be built, and what labour-saving devices could be introduced. She was a moving force in all his plans, particularly as they affected the lives and the interests of women and children. As the years passed and the village grew, husband and wife saw their dreams take shape in broad, tree-lined roads, in substantial red-brick houses and cottages, each set in its own garden, in shops, and church and Meeting House, Village Hall and children's schools, which were model buildings for their day. The modern student of architecture or the town-planner may lift his eyebrows superciliously at the Edwardian design, may query the whole concept of a garden city as a useful and æsthetically pleasing development. The modern social worker may mutter his doubts of paternalism —always a suspect activity unless exercised by the State. What both critics have to remember is the age in which Bournville was conceived, the background of Victorian housing conditions for the working classes against which it took shape, the squalor and dirt and poverty of the surroundings from which the tenants were brought to these new homes. Only with these considerations in mind can they begin to assess the value of this pioneer garden village.

As the houses were completed and the families, shy and a little awe-struck at the unfamiliar open spaces, the great sweeps of sky, the clean, freshly painted home, moved in, Elizabeth would come to welcome them, to learn their interests, and to help them find a niche in the village community. Similarly, whenever a baby was born she would be one of the first visitors to greet the little newcomer. If a household was stricken by death she would be there with a word of healing and some practical suggestion of sympathy—a quiet holiday at Wind's Point for the family, or some task to offer in the village community which would give the mourners a fresh interest and rouse them from the first stupor of grief.

It was the close, personal contact which she maintained with the tenants, so long as the size of the scheme rendered this practicable, that is remembered and cherished by the older inhabitants. That was Elizabeth's own particular contribution to Bournville. Others could have served the village in the administrative duties which she undertook after her husband's death, but none perhaps could have replaced her in those intimate, thoughtful tasks voluntarily assumed, though often by their nature so exacting of mind and spirit.

There were many other claims upon her time and energies in days that were becoming ever more crowded. The parties from the hot and dreary streets of the city, invited to share the peace and beauty of the Cadbury garden for a few hours, continued—their number, and the numbers of those attending them, increasing through the years. When the family removed to the Manor House in 1894 a large barn was built in the meadows near the entrance to the farm, where 700 people at a time could sit down to a meal. Caretakers were installed to organize the serving of teas, and throughout the spring and summer months, week by week, and sometimes almost day by day, the holiday-makers came flocking. Sunday schools from all parts of Birmingham, groups of crippled children, the members of the men's and women's Adult Schools, Mothers' Unions, and countless other societies would come to spend a day in the sun and fresh air. There were swings and seesaws for the children, a shallow brook chattering through the meadows where the hardy could paddle, and a bathing and boating pool for the older ones. Some would penetrate to the Manor gardens and pond, or crowd upon the terrace, where Mrs Cadbury, if at home, would always come to greet them with words of welcome and show them her loved flowers. In the last years of her life from twenty to thirty thousand people were thus visiting the Manor each summer. She would still, at ninety-two, walk down to the meadows to talk and joke with the children, to give a brief speech of welcome to the men and women who, through her hospitality, were free for a few hours of the strengthening quiet of the countryside.

In the early years of her marriage Elizabeth Cadbury's thought was much with the girls and young women who came into

Birmingham to work in shop, warehouse, or factory, and whose spare time was spent in dreary lodgings or wandering about the streets. The Y.W.C.A. was still a young movement (it had been formed in the year 1855), but was active both in the city, where there were fifteen branches alone, and in the county of Warwick. Shortly after her marriage Elizabeth Cadbury was asked to act as District Referee for all the branches included in the county, and threw herself whole-heartedly into the work. As the organization grew a Warwickshire District Council was formed, of which she became the first president.

One of the earliest problems which she tackled was that of finding suitable premises for a central hostel in Birmingham. There was in those days only one hostel within the precincts of the city, and that was situated in very poor and unsuitable premises in Cambridge Crescent. Elizabeth, driving one day through Corporation Street, noted that the building formerly occupied by the Conservative Men's Club was standing empty, though in a very dirty and dilapidated condition. But with her vision both of the likely needs of the Y.W.C.A. in future years and of what could be made of the gaunt structure before her, she saw at once that this was the place for the headquarters of the movement in the city. She took immediate action, travelling into Birmingham day by day by the slow transport of carriage or dog-cart to hammer out the terms of transfer and complete the purchase. The building, once taken in hand by a committee of the Y.W.C.A., proved readily adaptable to meet the growing and changing demands made upon it. It included eventually not only a hostel and a restaurant, but accommodation for a number of clubs and activities; for many years it was the home and the centre of friendship, of recreation, and of discussion for a large number of girls.

Elizabeth's connexion with the Y.W.C.A. was lifelong. When, in 1913, a reorganization of the national movement took place, and a Midland Division was formed, she became its first president, and held that office till 1936. The work took her to many centres within the Division for which she was responsible, advising, watching over the newly formed branches, giving especial attention to the needs of women and girls in wartime, both those remaining in civilian life and those serving with the Forces.

In 1936 a new Birmingham Division was formed in place of the Midland Union, of which Elizabeth was again made president, and Miss Eveleen Downes became the secretary; the latter had held the office of Secretary for the Midland Division since 1920. This close association between Elizabeth and her old friend and former secretary Miss Downes was a source of happiness and strength to both members of the partnership in their years of joint service for the Y.W.C.A.[1]

Elizabeth remained always sensitive to the changing needs of the girls of succeeding generations. She strove to get the organization run on more democratic lines when it was faced with the challenge of wartime conditions, and was one of those asked to send in a new draft constitution in 1916. In October 1918 there is a note in her journal that she had to attend, with other members of the Committee, at the Central Y.W.C.A. in Birmingham, meeting some of the girls who were boarding in the hostel, and who had been proving insubordinate. "As our conversation proceeded, my sympathies, I found, were with the girls rather than with the committee whom I was supposed to be backing. However, we managed a sort of compromise. Some of the girls asked if they might dance in the Lecture Hall before going to bed, so as to get warm. I saw objections rising on the faces of some present, so hastily said, 'Oh, yes, certainly, a nice healthy exercise.' I expect I shall hear about this at our next committee!" A few weeks later, attending the annual meeting of the Y.W.C.A. Council in Leeds, Elizabeth was much troubled over a threatened split in the organization "because dancing and other 'worldly' recreations are allowed at some clubs." She found it very difficult to maintain her patience and control her tongue at "the medieval outlook" of some of the members.

When the unavoidable parting of the ways came, and the extreme Evangelical section severed their ties with the Y.W.C.A.,

[1] A final change in the organization was made in 1946, when the Birmingham Division of the Y.W.C.A. became a City Association in a newly formed West Midland Division. Elizabeth Cadbury served the movement as President once more, both of the City Association and of the new Division.

Elizabeth continued her efforts resolutely on behalf of the main Association. In April 1939 a new Y.W.C.A. building was opened at Bordesley Green, in Birmingham, "the first really definitely recreative and educational building of its kind in the City." The Y.W.C.A. Committee, in Elizabeth's absence, decided to call the centre Dame Elizabeth House, as a recognition of all that she had done for the movement.[1]

Another opportunity to serve the girls of Birmingham was seized upon by Elizabeth when, in 1898, she formed the Birmingham Union of Girls' Clubs. At the time there were only three such clubs in existence in the city. But Elizabeth saw the greater strength and possibilities for service which would come to the movement through a closer contact between these groups of young people and their leaders. In the early years the activities of the Federation lay chiefly in a friendly competition in games, athletics, and dramatic performances; but opportunity was given for conference and discussion between the organizers of the clubs and their senior members. New clubs were formed, and the numbers within the union grew steadily year by year, including all types of groups. In May 1905, when she had been attending a competition of the Union of Girls' Clubs in the Town Hall, Elizabeth noted that it was eight years since the union was formed, "we began with a membership of 290 and it is now over 3000."

Twice in the course of the next half-century Elizabeth's fore-sight and her prompt and constructive action saved the Union from foundering at moments of crisis. Other cities gradually followed the lead of Birmingham, forming federations of their own, until in 1911 the Hon. Lily Montagu and Mrs Arnold Glover formed a National Council of Girls' Clubs. In 1927 Elizabeth handed over the running of the Birmingham Union to her daughter-in-law, Joyce Cadbury, wife of her son Laurence.

[1] The Centre was opened by her old friend Lady Aberdeen, the last public duty that the latter ever performed, for she died a fortnight later. Lady Aberdeen's last impression of Elizabeth Cadbury was of her undimmed vitality at the age of eighty-one, despite a fractured thigh. Her daughter, Lady Pentland, writing to Elizabeth Cadbury after her mother's death, said, "What impressed her on the visit to Birmingham was *your* marvellous activity. She told me how you stood up to receive and got about everywhere."

The Union in course of time became the Association and was later brought into line with the wider movement which developed into the National Association of Girls' and Mixed Clubs.

Elizabeth remained president of the Birmingham Association until 1944, and continued to watch with interest over its multifarious activities, including the organizing of training courses for club leaders, and the establishment of a country holiday home and conference centre at Windmill House, at Weatheroak, just outside the city boundary but in the "Green Belt" belonging to the Bournville Village Trust. The number of clubs affiliated to the Association has grown from the original three to one hundred and thirty, covering a great variety of organizations which attempt to foster the spiritual, educational, and physical welfare of the young people of the city.

Beyond these practical endeavours the active mind of Elizabeth was finding fresh fields to explore. The whole position of women was changing; many wives and daughters of prosperous middle-class citizens were no longer content to pass their days in a round of light household duties, social calls on their neighbours, and perhaps a few hours' visiting in the slums and distributing soup or calves-foot jelly to the sick. Even within the Society of Friends, where a rough equality between the sexes had been recognized from its foundation, the women members were demanding the right to take more part in its affairs. Hitherto, men and women had met separately in Monthly and Yearly Meetings to conduct the business of the Society, but though consultation took place on matters of importance affecting major changes in policy, on the whole the main guidance of the Society's work was in the hands of the Men's Yearly Meeting. No women were present on the executive committee of the Yearly Meeting, called the Meeting for Sufferings,[1] which gathered every month in London, and to which representatives came from Quarterly Meetings throughout the country. The women of Bristol and

[1] The name goes back to the early days of the Society when Friends often suffered persecution and imprisonment for their faith. The Meeting for Sufferings was concerned with the care of the men and women serving terms of imprisonment, and with taking any steps possible to ease the lot of the prisoners, and assuring them a just trial.

Somerset in 1884 were no longer prepared to accept this position and brought in a request to the Yearly Meeting that henceforth women should be recognized as forming a constituent part of all Quaker business meetings, including the executive committee. As a result of this plea, after some years of discussion, from 1898 women were included in the Meeting for Sufferings, and more and more joint sessions of the Yearly Meetings were held, until in 1907 the Women's Yearly Meeting was allowed to lapse. In these discussions and deliberations Elizabeth played her part and watched the outcome with much interest. In later life she served for many years on the Meeting for Sufferings, and only a few months before her death was still making her crisp and incisive contributions to that gathering.

Beyond the borders of her religious Society she was aware that on every hand women were awakening to a new sense of responsibility as members of the body politic, and were forming their own organizations to wrestle with problems of poverty, hunger, and disease at their source. Some, as a natural result of their desire to ease the suffering encountered in their social work, even wished to qualify as doctors. But when women wanted to use their brains, and were no longer satisfied with the earlier Victorian role of ministering angels, the storm broke. By the 'eighties, however, it had become obvious that, despite the prejudice and bitterness aroused in members of both sexes at the thought of women attacking the evils of society at their roots, irresistible forces were stirring. A conference on women's work, called in 1888 under the chairmanship of Lady Aberdeen, revealed what a variety and quantity of effort was being expended in attempts to improve conditions for women and girls both in industry and in the home and to lessen the volume of suffering. But there was much danger of wasting capabilities and resources through overlapping and duplication unless some system of co-ordination could be devised. Local unions of women workers were formed and regional conferences were held in the next few years, at which expert and voluntary social workers met and threshed out their problems together. Finally, in 1895, a new central body, a national Union of Women Workers, came into existence (which later took the name of the National

F

Council of Women), and a first Conference was held in Notting-ham under the presidency of Mrs Creighton, wife of the Bishop of Peterborough, and later of London.[1] Elizabeth Cadbury joined the Union in 1896, and continued as a member till her death in 1951. From 1898 to 1907 she was honorary treasurer—in those formative years when the organization was growing and developing rapidly, with the constant formation of new branches, the establishment of standing committees, and the affiliation of other already existing societies. In the years 1906 and 1907 she served as President of the National Union. Questions of housing, of industrial welfare, and, above all, of education were the main problems with which the early Union or Council was concerned. A large body of information was collected in the London office, which acted as a clearing-house for those seeking knowledge on these current problems, and an annual conference was held at which all branches were represented.

The purpose of the Conference, as Elizabeth saw it, "was for the members to find out better how to do their work, to give sympathy to and gain sympathy from those who differed in opinion and method but strove for the same end, to discover troubles that were as yet untouched, to learn how to avoid the multiplication of societies and committees and so avoid over-lapping and attain more efficiency," and "to gain experience, enthusiasm, faith, hope, and charity." She believed that the organization could be forged into an effective instrument for world peace, especially urgent as the threat of German naval expansion spurred on Great Britain to a race in armaments, but she realized clearly that peace could only be achieved if its founda-tions were laid in social justice. That was and remained her first concern. A few extracts from her presidential address of 1906 show the tenor of her thought at this time.

"William Penn said of George Fox that he 'was a match for every occasion' because he met the social and moral situations of his complicated epoch with a principle which almost invari-ably carried light and order unto them." It was this principle

---

[1] Mrs Sidney Webb, Lady Frederick Cavendish, Mrs Henry Fawcett, Mrs Henry Sidgwick, Mrs Arthur Lyttleton, Mrs Rawlinson, and Lady Laura Redding were among the first vice-presidents or members of the Executive.

that she sought herself and desired her fellow-workers to seek in the problems that confronted them.

After all, it is difficult to answer the question: Why is it that hundreds of thousands are born into circumstances where there seems no chance of leading healthy, useful, or desirable lives? Why was that soul, absolutely without choice, sent forth into those circumstances, that environment, to fight against such odds, with such poor equipment, with so often such a poor result? We want such conferences as ours to arouse in us a fresh desire to ask 'Why? Why?'

The usual reply to any suggestion that a time is coming when there may be equal chances for all is that, supposing all started fair to-day, there would be inequalities again to-morrow.

Certainly there would, but each would have had his opportunity. The circumstances that are shaped by the Divine power are of a different order; we recognize humbly and gladly the guiding hand of God and wait for the explanation some day of the questions that perplex us. But it is blasphemy to attribute to God the miseries and hardships of modern life caused by men's stupidity and selfishness.

As I pictured the great multitude of toiling women and children, and considered the conditions under which they live, their hopes and fears, their struggles, disappointments and failures, I thought of the prayer of George Fox; 'I prayed to God that He would baptize my heart into a sense of the needs and conditions of all men,' and as in measure that experience was granted, I was overwhelmed with thoughts of the puzzle of life, and the riddle of circumstance.

This was her cry. She saw many of her fellow-citizens who were at first prepared to question vigorously the existing social order and scale of values sink back into quiescence because no simple answer was forthcoming, or because they were baffled by the strongly entrenched position of privilege and custom. That was never to be the lot of Elizabeth Cadbury; to the end she would question and challenge, would seek patiently and persistently for the trail that led forward through the thickets of frustration and apathy, towards the solution of these wrongs. Want of thought, lack of imagination, fear of the cost—these were the things she attacked ruthlessly.

Above all, in the constantly growing round of activity, as she hurried from committee to committee, she never forgot that the people she encountered in conference and discussion, in the girls' clubs and hostels of the city, in her Adult School, and in her own kitchen were individual human beings, each with his peculiar needs and problems, capabilities and frailties. Perhaps one of her greatest gifts was her unfailing capacity to meet men and women, boys and girls, of all ages and classes, as persons, in whom she was genuinely interested, and in whom she had faith, however awkward, perverse, or feckless they might appear.

II

The final plunge into war with South Africa in October 1899 brought many Friends for the first time face to face with the implications of their historic peace testimony. The sympathies of Elizabeth and her husband were with the small Boer farmers, and they denounced the war as one of imperial aggression. Yet, as the slow years of the struggle dragged by, Elizabeth was aware, as many members of the Society were not, of the difficulties in her position. She realized that the mental eyesight, as she called it, of the majority of people was very dim, and often distorted. Where some, she realized, might see a clear light and a path to follow, to others all was darkness and confusion. The South African War must compel the thoughtful to admit that the intellectual equipment of the early twentieth century, on which more and more reliance was placed, was inadequate to give a clear vision or to point the way that would make for peace. All about her there was divergence of view and opinion in the men and women she encountered day by day. In her Quaker contacts she met constantly with people who believed that God had opened their eyes to see that all war was wrong and contrary to His will. But in her activities outside the Society she talked with others whom she equally respected and admired, who were mature in experience and wisdom, but who could not sincerely accept that position. Were Friends right, she asked, in claiming a clearness of vision, in thinking that they had been shown what was hidden from others, when often in their personal lives, or their business activities, they fell far short of the stupendous claim they were making? Along with many of her fellow-members, she discovered that the stand for peace could not be isolated from the claims of a fuller Christian witness in the day-to-day tasks. "We shall not . . . denounce war while we worship dividends," stated the Yearly Meeting of 1900 in an address which it issued to the nation.

It was criminal, said Elizabeth, to drift along secure in a shallow and selfish optimism which believed this to be the best of all possible worlds, either averting one's eyes from the suffering, the injustice, the disparities of wealth and poverty, that were to be found on every side, or accepting them, with a shrug, as inevitable. Some, she averred, even had the audacity to plead that the miserable conditions in which hundreds of their fellow creatures were condemned to pass their existence were the fault of the people themselves, or that, being used to such conditions, they did not mind them. In a great manufacturing centre such as Birmingham there was danger of too much time and energy being expended in money-making for its own sake, or of frittering wealth away in a round of pleasure-seeking. There was a danger that the whole powers of the mind might be given to the struggle for success in an earthly calling. If Friends were to put forward their peace testimony with conviction they could do it only with the humility that came from the knowledge of their temptations and failures in these and other directions. Elizabeth was quite clear that the testimony was but part of a vision of life, a daily practice and quality of living, that included all personal and social relationships, the choice of pursuits, the determination of values.

In 1900 the young Welshman Lloyd George, who was gaining a good deal of notoriety and abuse by his championship of the Boers and his opposition to the war, came to Birmingham to win the assistance of George Cadbury in obtaining control of a national daily newspaper which would voice the anti-imperial views of a section of the Liberal Party. George Cadbury, after some hesitation, contributed £20,000 towards the cost of purchasing The Daily News, Mr Thomasson of Bolton putting up a similar sum. A few years later Thomasson withdrew and eventually started The Tribune, and George Cadbury, to save the paper, assumed complete control of The Daily News.

From its early years, under George's direction, the paper took a line of its own. It was the vehicle for the peace party in the closing years of the Boer War; it organized an exhibition of sweated industries in 1906 which aroused public opinion to the needs of regulation and control, and which was visited by the future Queen Mary; it waged a campaign for granting compulsory powers to local authorities in the establishment of small holdings, which bore fruit in the Act of 1907. In all these causes Elizabeth maintained a keen, critical, and living interest, discussing the topics with her husband, watching the course of events day by day, always ready with timely and shrewd comment on the questions under consideration.[1]

[1] It was at Elizabeth Cadbury's suggestion that her stepson Henry went to Bouverie Street in 1907 to take over the management of the paper which had fallen on evil days financially. With the aid and the backing of his father, and of his older brother, Edward, and with the active co-operation of his brother-in-law, Bertram Crosfield, Henry Cadbury steered the paper through crisis after crisis. He retired in 1930 after *The Daily News* and *The Daily Chronicle* had merged, leaving the paper in a sound financial position and with an assured place in the country as one of the great London dailies, the mouthpiece of independent and liberal opinion.

8

Human Relationships in Industry and the Creation of the Bournville Village Trust

IN the spring of 1899, while on a visit to Egypt and Palestine, Richard Cadbury died suddenly in Jerusalem. Just before he set out on his travels the brothers had agreed that on the death of either the business should be converted into a limited company. So, with the passing of Richard Cadbury, the personal family business of sixty-eight years' standing was incorporated as Cadbury Brothers Limited, but the shares were still held by the members of the two families. George Cadbury became Chairman, and two of his sons and two of Richard's became managing directors of the new Company. These changes in structure, together with the growth of the factory, necessarily tended to weaken the earlier personal contacts between the directors and their workpeople. In the first years at Bournville, as the experiment of the new factory was tried and proved, the experience of the workers was that Richard and George Cadbury were trying to do something for them and with them, rather than trying to wring the last ounce of strength and effort from them. The employers got good service and full service, but they *attracted* it—they did not enforce it, this was the testimony of their people. The secret of skilled management and of leadership was theirs, though they probably would not have defined it in those terms or been able to expound clearly, save in the traditional phraseology of their Quaker faith, the principles which underlay their method of control.

The need to evolve some system of direct contact between management and workers in the large and still growing business, able to meet effectively changed circumstances and demands, was a problem weighing much upon George Cadbury and his fellow-directors as the new century opened. He would discuss such matters freely with his wife, for, though the factory as a business concern lay outside her sphere, anything which touched the welfare of the people employed was a matter of interest and of personal moment to her.

Though not, of course, herself responsible for any of the experiments or improvements adopted in the Bournville factory, from her knowledge of these she was able to grasp and make explicit in many public lectures and addresses given during the early years of the twentieth century certain guiding principles which, forty years later, have become basic factors in the science of management.

Elizabeth realized the difficulties and temptations that beset the girl who entered industrial life; she could appreciate the effect of factory discipline and routine on the health and character of the individual. These things, she urged, should be taken into account by the employer and should be matters for his thought and concern. There was much that he could do to stimulate the interest, to enrich the lives, of his work people. First, indubitably, she put the payment of a just and living wage. Any trade that did not comply with this demand "is a parasite upon the community," she said forthrightly in a public address of the year 1907. "The underpaid worker is subsidized by the rates and by the charitable, who are practically paying into the pockets of the unscrupulous employer. Perhaps as this is gradually understood legislation may be urged by the ratepayers in self-protection. For it is a humiliating fact that an appeal to self-interest sometimes brings a response not given to a plea for justice." But she saw that the responsibilities of the good employer did not end with the payment of an adequate wage. He could ensure that the physical conditions of his work-people were good—that the rooms in which their tasks were carried out were large, light, and well ventilated, that the sanitary arrangements were suitable and adequate, that nourishing, well-cooked food should be supplied in rooms set aside for this purpose. It must be remembered that up to the First World War it was the common practice for meals to be taken among the dirt and dust of the workshop. "The sickening smell of boiling oil and machinery is soon combined with the odour of frying bacon and herring," says a newspaper report of one Birmingham factory of the period. It was in contrast with such conditions that Cadbury Brothers had insisted upon a light and airy factory, upon separate dining-rooms and well-equipped cloakrooms for their people. "Work," said Elizabeth Cadbury, "is one of our greatest blessings, and not the curse of the Biblical story, but not too much of it." "The hours of labour," she urged, "should be limited to forty-eight a week [this was in 1907], and it should not be carried on in such an atmosphere that one's head is splitting within the first half-hour! Foremen and forewomen should be chosen for their character and gifts of leadership and not for their driving power."

Much might be done to alleviate monotony and to stimulate interest by encouraging the workers themselves to make suggestions about their daily tasks, their machines and materials; more still by the formation of works committees, in which the common problems affecting the life of the factory and its output could be discussed and handled by representatives of the management and the work-people. Such committees were in existence at the Bournville factory from the early years of the century, and Elizabeth drew on her knowledge of their procedure and success in urging others to adopt this method. Opportunities for education could be supplied by the establishment of evening schools; provision for organized games and gymnastics in leisure hours could be made by the employer who had the real care of his people at heart.

But there was still something more required, reaching beyond such measures of care and oversight, something intangible, which Elizabeth Cadbury found it difficult to put into words. "The good employer," she suggested, "can establish a feeling of sympathy and co-operation between himself and his people akin to the old family feeling that existed between the master and his apprentices in the days before machinery and huge industrial centres." Drawing on the experience of Bournville, she added, "I know an employer who created a friendly atmosphere when he had twenty workpeople and manages to maintain it still with five thousand." It could be done by that system of a shared responsibility which she saw exhibited in the early

Works Committees of the Bournville factory, by the inter-relationships established between the directors and their staffs and the men and women in the workshops. Above all, it could find expression in the attitude and bearing of the managers to their people, in the ultimate respect for the individual as a person who, by the fact of his humanity, is worthy of consideration and of fair and friendly dealing.

Beyond the walls of the factory and its problems were the homes of the people, the drab milieu in which their leisure was spent. Here, as Elizabeth Cadbury saw clearly, was a further responsibility resting upon the employer as a citizen. For the wealthy industrial magnate who spent most of his life in the country, far away from his business, knowing nothing of his people and their conditions, she had no time at all. Such people might give large sums to charity, but that did not absolve them. "By money gifts," said Elizabeth, with scorn, "they think to discharge their debt to mankind. Canon Barnett has well said, 'In God's army there are no substitutes.' The curse of absenteeism will have to disappear. An employer's first duty is to the men and women whose work has provided his wealth. . . . Most charitable institutions are demoralising," she continued. "Charity, meaning gifts of money and no personal interest, is not like mercy, it neither 'blesses him who gives nor him who takes.' It destroys the independence and manliness of the people who accept, and gives an undue sense of exaltation and superiority to the giver. What is needed is thoughtfulness, sympathy, justice. . . . Let us cease for a time trying to be kind and try to be just."

The housing conditions of the working classes in that first quarter of the twentieth century were "a disgrace to England; their dreary, unhealthy, crowded quarters are a menace to the health and morals of a large proportion of our population," she declared with trenchant vigour. The employers of labour, if they could not afford themselves to provide decent homes for their people, could at least try to meet the need through municipal enterprise and forethought. Was not the membership of Town and District Councils largely drawn from their ranks? Then, let them get busy. It was the lack of care, not the lack of opportunity, that prevented the problem from being tackled effectively.

Already she had arrived intuitively at the position which some modern writers on scientific management are stressing at the present day. For, from her intimate knowledge of people, her observation of their actions and reactions, she had realized that the domestic background of their lives, the conditions of their homes and their families, were all part of a complex of related facts, affecting the attitude of the workers at the bench, their energy, their capacity for concentration, their range of interests. No man or woman could rightly be considered as an isolated unit, "a hand," a mere cog in a machine. Each one was held in an intricate web of human relationships; those relationships in turn were affected by the facts of daily life in machine shop and factory, in office and warehouse. Each immediate group of fellow-workers was a living cell sensitive to the reactions of its members and so determining the pulse of life throughout the whole body.

Many of these ideas and suggestions put forward by Elizabeth and indicated in the quotations just given have become the current coin of thought and opinion. But in the day when she uttered them they were new-minted, startling and disturbing, far in advance of the thought of her age.

The Bournville Village Trust was created by George Cadbury in 1900, by which time the land he had bought was over 330 acres in extent and on part of which 300 houses were built by the end of that year. This estate and all his rights in it, amounting to a value of over £170,000, were handed over to a charitable Trust, whose object was to improve the housing conditions of the workers in and around Birmingham by giving them improved dwellings with gardens and open spaces. The Trust was empowered to buy, sell, or lease land, to build or to pull down and alter existing buildings, to borrow money, to give land for schools, hospitals, and other charitable purposes, to equip libraries, technical schools, and so on, to develop other estates, directly or indirectly, to join with other Trusts, companies, or private individuals in the management of property, to invest money, to employ staff, to make, alter, or repeal by-laws. Its administration was to be "wholly non-sectarian and non-political"; profits were not to be distributed, but were to be added to the Trust Fund and used for the promotion of its objects.

The announcement of what was in effect a gift to the nation of this magnitude brought much publicity to the village of Bournville. In the early years of the century visitors were flocking to it in growing numbers, many of them finding entertainment at the Manor House also for a meal, a night, or a week-end. A growing circle of friends and acquaintances was thus opened to Elizabeth Cadbury, from many walks of life and from many nations. It might be the Princess Marie Louise, entertained to lunch on the terrace, or Will Crooks, the Labour leader, who came for a week-end with his wife in October 1905, and wrote in his letter of thanks:

Speaking from us both it will be many a year if we ever forget your great kindness to us. You made us feel we were not out of place, a feeling I regret to say I do have in many houses I go to. I found with you food for reflection and thought, in a word, a new belief in the possibilities of what Christian employers could do, and how our Master's work is possible viz. Thy will be done on Earth as it is in Heaven.

It might be the French scholar and author of the *Life of St Francis,* M. Paul Sabatier, who arrived in June of the same year, just as a body of children from the schools in the neighbourhood were marching up to the door of the Manor to sing, after a day spent in the grounds. "M. Sabatier addressed them in French, George translating. The children were enchanted." Or it might be a party of German burgomasters, invited by her nephew-in-law, Barrow Cadbury, coming to get ideas for their own town-planning from the lay-out of Bournville.

In July 1905 John Burns came to address a large public meeting on the Bournville recreation ground, at which 10,000 were said to be present, and spent the week-end with the Cadburys. He read aloud to them the poems of John Markham on the Sunday evening, and on Monday afternoon, when the annual gathering of the Severn Street, Northfield, and Selly Oak Women's Adult

Schools was held at the Manor, mustering some 600 mothers and children, he spoke to them also, to their great delight.

In September Walford Davies[1] was a guest at Sunday supper. (It was the practice of George and Elizabeth to collect a heterogeneous number of guests on Sunday evening, and the supper table was always a scene of keen discussion.) Walford Davies was then organist at the Temple Church in London, and the family listened to his playing on Elizabeth Cadbury's organ through an evening that passed all too rapidly. Albert Schweitzer was another visitor who, in later years, enjoyed playing that organ.

Charles Masterman, after a visit in November of 1905, said in his letter of thanks to Mrs Cadbury: "Bournville itself went far towards the realization of a dream which I had not imagined that I should ever see in tangible form in this queer and complicated world."

Mrs Gilbert Keith Chesterton added her tribute when members of the staff of the *Daily News* had enjoyed the hospitality of the Manor House for a week-end. G. K. Chesterton had entertained the household with his brilliant sketches on the evolution of the warming-pan, George Cadbury's favourite cure for a cold, from which he was suffering, and which was seen by Chesterton for the first time in operation.[2] "I must write a line to-night, though it is very late (real journalistic hours) to thank you for the very delightful week-end we spent with you. We feel much invigorated at the thought of the life going on around you and can now even dare to dream of a whole England planned on Bournville lines. The whole thing was a revelation to us." And one correspondent at least saw the value of even one such practical experiment in the midst of the theoretical web-spinning of the political parties: "One hopes that so many examples of goodwill and effort cannot fail to stimulate others. Really it is a very great help to see your life at your house, and the Adult Schools, and Bournville. One sees so little of the kind in political

[1] Sir Walford's sister was for some years employed at the Bournville factory.

[2] George Cadbury believed so firmly in the efficacy of the warming-pan that he kept a supply in the Bournville Estate office which tenants going into their newly built houses might borrow, to ensure that they would not sleep in damp beds.

or social life and among all the vague and timid ways that are the fashion, it is all the more valuable to us who visit you."

Bournville was exerting a wider influence on the course of town-planning in England. In September 1905 George and Elizabeth, with their daughters Isabel and Eleanor, visited the site of the new Garden City at Letchworth, in Hertfordshire, where Elizabeth presided over a Women's Housing Conference. Many Friends were both personally and financially interested in the formation of the First Garden City Company Limited, which promoted the develop-ment of Letchworth, and on this visit the Cadbury's encountered several of their fellow-Quakers driving round the site and inspect-ing the cottages already erected. The ideas carried out in the build-ing of Bournville had much influence on the Letchworth planners.

The later enterprise of Hampstead Garden Suburb, in which Canon and Mrs Barnett were so greatly concerned, was also developed with Bournville in mind; Mrs Barnett was wont to refer to it as "the grandchild of Bournville."

Walter Runciman, Under-Secretary to the Local Government Board, came to Bournville in 1906 to see the village and to discuss housing conditions with George and Elizabeth, before framing the Government's first Housing Bill. The Bournville architects throughout the last half-century have given much help and advice to those promoting housing schemes in other localities, and in later years to the Birmingham Copec[1] House Improvement Society Ltd., which has done so much to recondi-tion some of the houses in Birmingham, pending demolition under slum-clearance schemes. Many members of different municipal authorities have come to the Estate throughout the years to seek inspiration in planning fresh districts of their own, so that the spark of vision which lit the minds of George and Elizabeth has kindled a fire to sweep away the crowded slums of our towns and cities, and to set in their places homes of a new standard for the people of the nation.

---

[1] Copec, the Conference on Politics, Education, and Citizenship, held in Birmingham in 1924. Its more recent enterprises include a two-storey block of flats for single women and a block of self-contained apartments for elderly people in need of some medical and nursing care, but not so incapacitated as to warrant removal to hospital or nursing-home.

II

Within the Society of Friends also new currents of thought were sweeping into the Evangelical strongholds. The younger generation, under the leadership of such men as John Wilhelm Rowntree, William Charles Braithwaite, Edward Grubb, and many others, were beginning to rediscover for themselves the living, mystical basis of their faith. A turning-point in the Society's history was reached in the Manchester Conference of 1895, which George and Elizabeth attended. Here, for the first time, an attempt was made to assess, in the light of modern thought, the Quaker experience of the living God revealed in the human spirit, and to consider the implications of that faith in terms of the social order, the current business morality, and the new political relationships in Britain. Out of the Conference grew the Summer School Movement for further study. Biblical exegesis, the history of Nonconformity and particularly of the early Quaker movement, a consideration of modern developments in religious and theological thought—these and kindred subjects were lectured upon by able scholars to large audiences of Friends, and eager discussions followed the lectures.

Three large summer schools were held, each lasting for some weeks, between 1897 and 1901, two of them at Scarborough and one at Birmingham (1899). Elizabeth attended the Scarborough gatherings, but was particularly active at the Birmingham School, helping with the arrangements beforehand, attending lectures and discussions, bringing out parties of students for entertainment at the Manor and to see something of Bournville.

To the young men and women of the Society, and to many of its more mature members, this movement brought an entirely new angle of vision upon men and events. For they found that the knowledge of God depended not on the belief in the unchallengeable truth of all Scriptural statements, nor on the magical efficacy of the physical blood of Christ shed for the sins of the world, but on the stirring and impulse of the divine life moving in the heart and mind of man, on a reality which could be discovered in worship and contemplation and the truth of whose leadings could be tested in action. It was a vital, challenging, joyous faith, opening up new continents of thought and experience to the Quakers of that day, who for the most part had been reared in the strait jacket of rigid Evangelical doctrine. They "discovered for the first time that it was possible to be a Christian and an open-minded seeker after truth," says Edward Grubb, who took a prominent part as a lecturer in this movement.[1]

John Wilhelm Rowntree, though threatened with growing blindness and loss of hearing, was by 1897 occupied with the idea of a more sustained effort in religious education for the younger members of the Society, of which the Summer Schools were merely the forerunner. He, with many other Friends, was much troubled by the poor quality of the ministry in the Quaker Meetings for Worship. "We want the imagination that springs from sympathy and the freshness that springs from thought," he wrote in 1904. "To deal in the obvious because thinking is too much trouble is to offer unconsecrated ministry." And again, "Let it be acknowledged that the problem of the Free Ministry is not only a spiritual but a practical one. We have it yet to solve. There are needs of the human heart which are not met by prophecy and exhortation, but by teaching, and the ministry of teaching demands a trained and ordered mind."[2]

At London Yearly Meeting in 1901, while speaking of the need for increased study and intellectual vitality, he first publicly outlined his dream of a Quaker college or residential educational settlement, which would carry on more thoroughly and more fundamentally the work begun in the Summer Schools. A few months later, while out for his customary morning ride before breakfast, it was borne in upon George Cadbury that he should offer his house, Woodbrooke, for this purpose.

Months of discussion and planning followed, and the Manor House became the rendezvous for those interested in the project and prepared to give time and effort to its realization. Joshua Rowntree, Edward Grubb, Henry Lloyd and Theodora Wilson, William Littleboy, John William Hoyland, John

[1] *Friends Quarterly Examiner*, October 1938, No. 288, p. 307.
[2] *Palestine Notes and other Papers*, by John Wilhelm Rowntree, "On Lay Ministry," pp. 112 and 114.

George Cadbury
Eliz. M. Cadbury
June 19ᵗʰ 1888 to June 19ᵗʰ 1913

A SILVER WEDDING PICTURE
June 19, 1913.
Photo Harold Baker

WOODBROOKE, SELLY OAK

Elizabeth Cadbury's home from her marriage in 1888 until 1894.
This was the first of the Selly Oak Colleges.

THE MANOR HOUSE, NORTHFIELD

Her home from 1894 until her death. (Now a students' Hall of
Residence for Birmingham University.)

Photo G. F. Charlton

Henry Barlow, Henry Stanley Newman, M. Catherine Albright, Richard Thomas, of Baltimore, and Rufus Jones, of Haverford, Pennsylvania—these were among the stalwarts of Quakerism who gathered at the Manor for long week-ends of steady work and planning. On April 18, 1903, some fifty Friends met there in conference, at which John Henry Barlow, Secretary of the Bournville Village Trust, laid before them the matured suggestions of the earlier groups. The house and grounds of Woodbrooke were given by George and Elizabeth Cadbury, and their maintenance was guaranteed by them. In addition, George Cadbury set aside a sum of £12,000 in preference shares in the *Daily News* to endow a lectureship. He also offered a number of scholarships open to all Friends during 1904 for boys and girls who had left school within the last five years. Each scholarship covered one term's residence at Woodbrooke, including the payment of railway fares from the student's home to Birmingham.

In the discussion which greeted the proposal Friend after Friend expressed their sympathy with the originators, and the new hope for the life of the Society which it promised. "Very satisfactory—all seemed very pleased," runs Elizabeth's diary for that day. "Many schoolmasters attend. Gulielma Crosfield, Gertrude Ellis, Esther Seebohm, Claude [Elizabeth Cadbury's brother], F. M. Brown, William Charles Braithwaite, and Arnold Rowntree to town in motor and waggonette. Very tired in evening, but feel it a great success."

It was decided to open the settlement by a summer school, which began on July 22, 1903, with an inaugural address by Rufus Jones, who had come over from America for the express purpose of attending it. He and his wife landed in England on July 18, to be met by a cablegram saying that their little son Lowell, at home in the United States, was seriously ill. They reached the Manor at 9.30 on Sunday, the 19th, and had by then received the news that their son had died the previous Thursday.

Elizabeth, busy with arrangements for the Summer School and the opening of Woodbrooke, and with many guests to entertain while it was held, laid all aside to meet the emergency. The afternoon she spent walking round and round the garden

G

in talk with the stricken father, and found herself deeply impressed with the beauty of his spirit. Rufus Jones, with great courage, decided to stay a fortnight and to give his lectures rather than disappoint his audience. Rufus Jones and John Wilhelm Rowntree both stayed at the Manor during the School; even Elizabeth noted that with all her guests and her family it was "a crowded house."

In August, while a second session of the School still continued, she left with her family for a holiday at Cromer, and here Rendel Harris arrived on August 25, two days after his return from Armenia where he had been working for the resettlement of the victims of the Turkish persecution. He came "to talk over Woodbrooke, and inclines to go there," says Elizabeth Cadbury, "to act as Director of Studies, giving up the Queen of Holland's invitation to accept the Chair of Theology at Leyden." By the end of October Woodbrooke was fairly launched on its career, with an enthusiastic group of students under the direction of Rendel Harris, and with Joshua and Isabella Rowntree as wardens.

At first the management of the Settlement was left to the Summer School Continuation Committee, the Trustees appointed by the Deed of Foundation reserving to themselves the control and responsibility for all alterations and repairs of the buildings and the upkeep of the grounds. In 1906 a new Committee of Management was nominated, with power to appoint or discontinue its own members in future, and Elizabeth and George were active members of this body. A year later the two committees were merged in the Woodbrooke Council, on which Elizabeth served throughout her life.

Woodbrooke itself had many criticisms to face. The very idea of any form of training for the Ministry was abhorrent to the more conservative Friends; theology and the Higher Criticism were anathema to the strong Evangelical section of the Society. A large influx of students from Holland, who came to hear Rendel Harris in England, as they had failed to tempt him to Leyden, threatened at first to swamp the English students. The close connexion with the Low Countries has always been maintained, and when a new men's hostel came to be built in 1906 it was named Holland House in honour of the substantial contingent from that country always to be found among the students. A staff of able lecturers in Biblical Scholarship, Quaker History, Economics, and English Literature was assembled in the early terms, including, besides Rendel Harris himself, Robert S. Franks,[1] A. Neave Brayshaw, Tom Bryan, and George Shann. Quietly and steadily the work went forward, and Woodbrooke through the years won for itself a place of recognition in the Society.

If, with changing needs, it has not kept rigorously to the original purposes and the deep concern of its founders, it yet remains a unique institution in this country. People of many nationalities, of varying creeds or none, from the late 'teens to the sixties, gather for courses of study in religious subjects and the social sciences. To many it is the place where new windows are opened on to the world in which they live, where friendships are formed between oddly assorted people, where understanding of different ways of thought, different traditions of life and custom, are first conceived.

Around Woodbrooke also sprang up a number of institutions with differing purposes, but sharing to some extent in the life of lecture hall and common room.

The earliest was Kingsmead, for the preparation of missionaries entering into Quaker service abroad, and Westhill, for training kindergarten and Sunday-school teachers in new methods which relied greatly on handwork and visual aids to knowledge. They were opened in 1905 and 1906 respectively, Westhill under the guidance of George Hamilton Archibald, a Canadian, whose Sunday school, held in the Ruskin Hall at Bournville, was visited at week-ends by people from all over the British Isles. Elizabeth's youngest sister, Josephine, who had spent some years in missionary work and nursing in Armenia and the Central Provinces of India, married the warden of Kingsmead, John William Hoyland, in 1906.[2] Together husband and wife built up a home for their

---

[1] Father of Sir Oliver Franks, late British Ambassador to Washington.

[2] Josephine Taylor was his second wife, and she had the care of his two young sons, Jack and Geoffrey Hoyland. Geoffrey, after the First World War, was to marry Elizabeth Cadbury's own daughter, Dorothea, thus forging a double link between the two families.

students and an enlightened course of training for work in the Mission field.

In 1909, on the initiative of George Cadbury, junior, and of Tom Bryan, the economics lecturer at Woodbrooke, a residential college for working men was opened and was named Fircroft. It was modelled on the Folk High Schools of Denmark, which George Cadbury had studied at first hand. In the course of the next thirty years other foundations of other religious denominations were opened in the neighbourhood, so that by the inter-war period some ten colleges were in existence as centres of adult education and religious instruction, all linked together in the Senate of the Selly Oak Colleges. Several also maintained a close association with the University of Birmingham. They stand somewhat apart from any similar institutions in the country as a training ground for men and women in social and theological studies.

The advance of secondary and technical education in the country generally, which had lagged behind that of the Continent, was greatly aided by Balfour's Education Act of 1902. This measure swept away the old school boards, and handed over the responsibility for both elementary and secondary education to the County Councils and the County Boroughs, working under the ægis of the Board of Education. It aroused bitter opposition in Nonconformist circles, as Balfour strengthened the financial position of church schools by putting them on the rates. The breach opened in the ranks of Liberal Nonconformity by the different attitudes adopted towards the Boer War was largely healed in a common resistance to the new measure. Some Nonconformists, including a few Friends, felt so strongly on the matter that they refused to pay the education rate, and suffered distraint of their goods. The Free Church Council entered the political field as a rallying-point of the opposition, an action deprecated by both George and Elizabeth Cadbury. They resigned from the Council, and Elizabeth in a letter to her brother Claude made her views clear. Most Nonconformists, she felt, were in danger of interfering, without sufficient thought or consideration, in political questions, forgetting that they were religious communities. Though their religious faith would of course influence and inform the political beliefs and actions of men and women, in every Church if it were a living communion all shades of political belief would be represented, and the Church as such could not rightly take action or broadcast statements on issues of party politics. She welcomed the opportunities offered by the Act to the able child of any class who would henceforth, by a system of scholarships, be enabled to climb the educational ladder from primary school to university, and announced firmly that she "extremely objected" to the passive resisters.

The early twentieth century was a period when the doctrine that the spread of education would prove a panacea for most social evils was coming to the fore. It was with particular delight therefore that Elizabeth turned her attention to the building of the Bournville Village Schools, which were opened on April 23, 1906. On the opening day 420 children turned up for enrolment, and the need of additional teachers was a first cry of the staff. The District Council had refused the number originally suggested on the ground that they did not believe the school would be full enough to justify these appointments. For the next few weeks Elizabeth was working indefatigably to overcome the difficulties and supply the deficiency. The building had been designed with classrooms which would hold only thirty to forty children, to avoid the evils of excessively large classes, but on account of the shortage of staff seventy-five or eighty were of necessity placed under one teacher in those opening weeks. By the end of the month, however, the committee had engaged two more permanent and three temporary teachers. "We still require three more permanent teachers before our staff will be anything like sufficient," wrote Elizabeth. "The niggardly District Councils, however, will only allow the extra teachers uncertificated, and we have had to refuse two very good applications on this account."

It must be remembered that these activities took place only a few weeks before the birth of her last child, Ursula, on May 20, when Elizabeth herself was within a month of her forty-eighth birthday.

An Infants' School was added to the main building in 1910, the little Ursula laying the foundation-stone. The Bournville

Schools remained always a particular concern of Elizabeth's. It was a continuing pleasure to her to attend the morning assembly, even to the last weeks of her life, and say a few words to the children before they dispersed to their classes. At ninety-two she could still capture and hold their interest on a morning of brilliant February sunshine, when there was every excuse for a child's attention to stray and for small limbs to fidget. But the little crowd, standing in the hall with their eyes fixed on the unbowed figure of Dame Elizabeth, were eager to catch every word as she questioned them about the flowers already opening in their gardens at home, and urged them to be alert to the new beauties yet to be discovered day by day in the weeks ahead. Something of the zest of living, of the exciting enjoyment of simple things which would turn each day into an adventure, passed from the old lady to the youngest child in her audience.

Elizabeth's interest in education found also another field of expression in the meetings of the "Mothers in Council" in Birmingham, which she attended most faithfully. These were small and informal gatherings of parents who were concerned with the difficult question of the right and healthy upbringing of their children. The Parents' National Education Union had been formed about the same time, and some years later the Birmingham group of Mothers in Council was invited to join this society and eventually did so. Elizabeth maintained her interest and gave her active co-operation to the work of the P.N.E.U., acting as President of the Birmingham branch for some years; she engaged a governess for her youngest daughter who had been trained in their methods.

Bournville itself was developing rapidly in these years. New shops were opened, the gardens were maturing and were a brilliant sea of colour in the spring and early summer; hundreds of people would come out from Birmingham on a Sunday to stroll through the broad roads and open spaces and enjoy this unaccustomed beauty. In late August 1905 the Friends' Meeting House at Bournville was finished, and the first meetings were held there on September 2 and 3. As this was the only place of public worship in the Village for some years, George and Elizabeth Cadbury were anxious to meet the needs of non-Quaker attenders. For this purpose certain modifications of Friends' customary usage were introduced; there were always at least two hymns, towards the beginning and end of the Meeting, and a Bible reading early in the Meeting before it finally settled into silent waiting before God. These practices were continued throughout the years. It was characteristic of Elizabeth's generosity of spirit that when, in the latter years of her life, the younger members of the Meeting asked that the Bible reading should be discontinued, feeling that it had become a formal and stereotyped practice, she agreed, though regretfully, and accepted the change with good grace.

On Tuesday, September 26, 1905, Elizabeth tells us "we had our first Congregational Meeting at the new Meeting House at Bournville; a large number of people attended. About sixty were placed on a provisional Committee for managing the work of the congregation; this will be divided up into about seven sub-committees. . . . We are not yet a recognised Friends' Meeting, as we wish the application to come from the congregation itself. Everybody seems to like the Meeting, and there is a very pleasant feeling of unity amongst those who come, though they comprise Presbyterians, Anglicans, Wesleyans, Congregationalists, Plymouth Brethren, and Friends, also, I believe, a Baptist. We intend to have an associate membership which anyone can join without actually becoming a member of the Society, or leaving their own denominations."

The Meeting for Worship at Bournville was henceforth the centre of Elizabeth's religious life; every Sunday, morning and evening, she attended it faithfully when at home, taking a leading part in the vocal ministry. Her contributions were nearly always connected with some event of the week with which she had been concerned, some experience encountered in her dealings with people in the course of her many activities, but right to the end remained lucid, clear-cut, and incisive—never lapsing into the long and rambling discourse which is so often characteristic of the elderly speaker. Above all they were rooted in her clear and living faith in the goodness and the guidance of God.

9

Welfare of Children and Youth

IN the first fourteen years of the twentieth century three new features appeared in the pattern of English life. These were the rise of a growing suburban population made possible by improved means of transport, the appearance of the cheap, popular newspaper, and, more intangible, the growth of a strange hysteria and bitterness in public life. If the closing decade of Victoria's reign had been dominated by the Irish question, and by a new militant imperialism in the scramble for African territory, the opening decade of the new century was overshadowed by the shift of the balance of power in Europe and the rapid extension of Germany's naval forces. At home a rising standard of living and such advanced measures of social security as the introduction of old-age pensions and a system of health and, in certain trades, of unemployment insurance, were accompanied or followed by an outbreak of industrial strife which contained a new bitterness and threat of violence and culminated in the great railway strike of 1911 and the coal strike of 1912. A more militant patriotism, sensationalism ("the love of excitement without danger"), the questioning of Victorian standards and shibboleths, the movement for Protection as against free trade, openly voiced by Joseph Chamberlain in the early years of the century—this was the temper, these the vague ideas, that stirred in the minds of the pre-1914 generation.

The political landslide which brought the Liberals to power in 1906 appeared to Elizabeth, as to many others in the country, to open a new age of hope and promise. In a family letter written at that time she says:

Wilfrid rather jeers at the time of prosperity which he thinks the Liberals immediately expect to settle down over England on account of their victory, but I think if he knew some of the younger men who have gone into Parliament this time as we do, with most keen desire to help the people and detachment from party politics as such, he would think there was much more hope than there has ever been before.

The quotation suggests that one of the great ills of the next half-century—the growing domination of politics by rigid party creeds—was seen thus early by Elizabeth. But she could not foresee the shattering of her hopes by the attitude of the Upper Chamber in its persistent blocking of Government legislation, which was to lead to the great constitutional crisis of 1909–1910.

A new field of opportunity and service was opened to Elizabeth by the educational programme of the Liberal Government. In 1907 it placed upon local authorities the duty of providing for the medical inspection of children under their care either immediately before, or just after, their admission to an elementary school. A further clause granted them the power (as distinct from the duty) "to make such arrangement as may be sanctioned by the Board of Education for attending to the health and physical condition of the children educated in public elementary schools."[1]

The Act came into force in Birmingham on September 1, 1908. A School Medical Officer was appointed, together with three assistants and three nurses. Their work was at first confined to the medical inspection of children on their admittance to the schools; it was not until 1912 that any move was made towards a greater care for the health and physical condition generally of the child throughout its school career. In the shaping and direction of that wider service within the city Elizabeth was to play a leading part.

For some years she had served on the Worcestershire Education Committee, gaining valuable experience in methods of local government and the problems of the school service. In 1911, after much discussion and very much against the wishes of many inhabitants dwelling on its outskirts, Birmingham, by an Order

[1] Education (Administrative Provisions) Act, 1907, Section 13 (1), (b).

of the Local Government Board, absorbed within its administrative boundaries some of the sprawling suburbs, including Kings Norton, Northfield, and Selly Oak,[1] and these henceforth became part of a "Greater Birmingham."

Elizabeth was invited to serve on the City Education Committee after these arrangements came into force, and in November 1911 attended the first meeting of the new and enlarged body. A month later, to her great surprise, she was invited to act as chairman of the Hygiene Sub-committee, set up by the City Education Committee, and agreed to accept this responsibility. With characteristic energy and thoroughness she then launched a whole series of inquiries, by letter and personal interview, to discover all she could of the possibilities entailed in this new task, and enjoyed particularly the opportunity of consulting her friend Sir George Newman, then Chief Medical Officer at the Board of Education, and reaping the benefit of his experience and wisdom.

An immediate task was to interview various hospitals, urging them to allow the Education Authority to institute clinics for the treatment of school children on their premises. On March 26, 1912, Elizabeth tells us, she visited the Dental Hospital in company with other members of the Committee, and went all over it, "seeing various people in various stages of agony." The officials of the hospital agreed to rent to the Hygiene Sub-committee a whole floor, with all the dental equipment, for five afternoons a week. Encouraged by this friendly co-operation, the deputation went on to a second interview at another hospital, where their experience was just the reverse. "The hospital committee, for some reason, appeared to object to any treatment being given at all, then said the Board of Education was not competent to deal with such cases, and next that their hospital was already doing all that was necessary. I only knew one of the doctors . . . who was very fiery; he more or less apologized to me afterwards and asked how I liked managing a committee composed almost entirely of men. I told him I did not mind so long as they knew how to behave."

[1] Bournville was mainly in Kings Norton, but parts were (and are) in the other two suburbs.

Despite the difficulties, the newly constituted committee went forward undaunted under the energetic leadership of its chairman. The enlarged city was divided into six areas for the purposes of the school medical service, with six assistant medical officers and nine nurses to staff them. "Our scheme for the treatment of school children went through the Education Committee," notes Elizabeth in May 1912, after she had laid before it ably and succinctly her committee's programme. Treatment for the minor ailments of school children, including the provision of spectacles, was carried out at the six inspection centres established in different parts of the city, each of which served the neighbouring schools. Each was equipped with a dark-room to aid in testing eyesight by estimating errors of refraction, and a part-time ophthalmic surgeon was appointed in the spring of 1913. Dental treatment did not begin till early in 1913, but five dental clinics were opened in the course of that year, and some 6500 children passed through these centres during the twelve months. "I bought toys, bricks, and books which I am going to take to the three centres where dental treatment of school children begins to-day," wrote Elizabeth to the absent members of her family on January 7, 1913. She hoped that if the children had some pleasant occupation while waiting to see the dentist they would want to come again to enjoy the toys!

Another new departure, which lay very near to the heart of Elizabeth and for which she battled unwearyingly, was the building of a Central School Clinic in Great Charles Street, adjacent to the Dental Hospital. Coupled with this was a scheme for adapting the Education Offices at Handsworth as a hospital for the treatment of tonsils and adenoids, where children could spend a night after the operation instead of being sent home immediately, still suffering from shock and loss of blood. It was a great blow to her when the Committee refused to go forward with these schemes, becoming frightened at the expenditure involved. But she refused to allow her dream to die. In January 1913 the Central Clinic and the hospital for adenoidal operations again appeared on her agenda. A meeting of the Chairmen of all sub-committees of the Education Committee was held annually to consider their plans and expenditure in the coming year; Elizabeth Cadbury was the only woman present on this occasion among some twelve business-men. She refused to reduce her Committee's budget, and suggested that all the committees should resign in a body, rather than scale down their plans, and invite the Council to find a fresh set of people, if it were possible, who could do the work better and more cheaply. At the end of the month she had the pleasure of seeing her scheme pass the full Education Committee and go forward to the City Council. On February 25, while she was at Bordighera, she received a telegram from her stepson George to say that it had been accepted by that body.

In the early autumn Elizabeth was busily engaged in discussing the plans for the new clinic with the Education Committee's architect. "I have got baths included, and also cooking apparatus," she writes triumphantly, "so that we may be able to supply waiting mothers with tea, and perhaps at some future stage have simple cooking demonstrations and health talks." By September 1915, even before it was opened, she was making arrangements for the cooking demonstrations to be held. The clinic was planned to include examination, treatment, and waiting-rooms, and was equipped with an X-ray apparatus. For the choice of decoration and furnishing Elizabeth was largely responsible; the building was finally completed and was opened by Sir George Newman on September 23, 1915.

The second part of Elizabeth's plan also came to fruition in 1913. On October 13 she writes that she had been to Handsworth

where our clinic for operations on throats and adenoids was opened for the first time. The rooms are quite charming; we have the old Handsworth Education Offices, and the Board Room, panelled with oak, is used as a ward, in which are ten beds surrounded by screens, where the children are to be kept for twenty-four hours after the operation. I went in with the children and saw them directly afterwards. I thought my being there might give the parents confidence, but it was a rather gruesome sight.

During the next few years the number of school clinics grew to twelve, and the medical staff increased rapidly. The visits of the medical officers to the schools were much more frequent than heretofore, enabling them to keep a check on the course of treatment advised in particular cases. The doctors, being allocated to one region, came to know the parents and were able to win their trust. Revised methods of inspection had been initiated, the medical officers making their examinations at the schools in the mornings, and then attending at the clinic with two nurses every afternoon to carry out the necessary treatment. It was found that this plan was welcomed both by teachers and parents; by the teachers, because school work was less disturbed by a regular morning inspection than it had been when this took place indiscriminately morning and afternoon, and by the parents, because they knew for a certainty that each clinic would be open every afternoon, and the mothers, many of whom were compelled to go out to work in the mornings, could bring their children to the clinics for advice, re-examination, and treatment when they were held later in the day. The thought given to such apparently minor details, which yet made all the difference in the smooth running and efficiency of the service, is typical of Elizabeth's very practical vision of the needs of a situation.

Her keen and prolonged interest in the school medical service over a period of twenty years was focused not merely on the children passing under its care, but also on the conditions of life to which women and children were subjected during the twenty-four hours of the day. "Boys and girls are being spoilt physically, mentally, and morally by their too early emergence into the ranks of the employed, by lack of guidance in the choice of occupations suited to their capacity, by inadequate opportunities of skilled training, and by insufficient safeguarding and husbanding of their physical powers and resources," she said in a lecture on Public Health delivered in 1913:

Medical inspection, medical treatment, and school hygiene in its largest sense should be brought into direct application in relation to industry. . . .

An Authority which desires to do what is best for the child while he is at school is driven to take into account both the influences which affect the child before he comes to school, and the conditions and circumstances of employment which he will have to face when he leaves school and for which the school is to prepare him. . . .

It cannot be too clearly understood that school hygiene and school treatment, not to speak of education in its largest sense, rest upon a right understanding and appreciation of the physical character and needs of the individual child.

In the course of her work for the Council she also served on the body of School Managers responsible for schools in the south-west of Birmingham, a group of which Sir George Kenrick, Norman Chamberlain, and George Cadbury, junior, were also members. She spent much time in visiting the schools and serving on Attendance Committees to inquire into the causes of absence. "The parents who have not sent their children to school, or those who require free breakfasts for their children, have to come before one of the Attendance Committees to give evidence and have their cases decided. It is always rather a melancholy business, especially in seeing the shiftiness and shiftlessness of some of the parents. A few cases are very pathetic, but one feels so helpless in not being able to follow them up," she tells us, and confesses that she leaves these meetings "absolutely fagged out."

A second field of educational activity in which Elizabeth was keenly interested was that of the Day Continuation Schools for young workers in industry. The first to be established in Birmingham—and perhaps in the country—grew out of the classes for their own young employees started by Cadbury Brothers Limited largely on the initiative of George Cadbury, junior. Another firm, Morland and Impey, joined in, and in 1913 the City Education Authority agreed to maintain a school whose object was to continue the general education of youths and girls in industry; for this purpose they were to be released from employment without loss of wages for (usually) the equivalent of one day a week until they reached the age of at least eighteen. The late H. A. L. Fisher embodied compulsory provisions on the Bournville model in the 1918 Education Act, but for economy reasons they were never fully implemented nationally. Birmingham, London, and Rugby were the three cities which adopted the scheme. The Bournville School (and some others) continued, and the scheme for "County Colleges" embodied in the 1944 Education Act again derived in a considerable degree from the pioneer work of Birmingham. The Bournville

School was later renamed Day Continuation College by the Birmingham Education Authority—who continued to staff, administer, and finance it—and it is now attended by some 1800 young people drawn from sixty firms and from Government and municipal departments. 'Day release,' as it is called, while not yet statutorily established, is in force in many parts of the country.

Elizabeth Cadbury's interest was chiefly from the angle of her membership of the Education Committee and not, of course, as an employer. But the possibility of further education for the young worker was a project after her own heart, and for the next years she was busy on many occasions giving public addresses on the work of the schools and rousing enthusiasm for embarking on further experiments in this direction. The economies introduced in the post-1918 years, curtailing the extension of educational facilities and cutting off the provision for Day Continuation Schools, she described as "one of the most pernicious mistakes ever perpetrated by an irresponsible reactionary government."

In all its aspects, education was a cause into which she threw her energies unsparingly. In recognition of all that she had done in this direction Birmingham University awarded her the honorary degree of M.A. in 1919. She was a keen member of the Child Study Association, acting as president of the Birmingham Branch in 1916; she was president of the Birmingham and Midland Home and School Council formed in that year; she was a member of the Birmingham section of the Parents' National Education Union, and presided at a Conference of Educational Institutions called by that organization in Birmingham in 1909, at which Lord Lytton, the chairman of the parent society, was the speaker. She was one of the foundation members of the Board of Governors of Birmingham University, founded by Royal Charter in 1900, and at the dinner held in 1950 to commemorate the half-century of the University's existence she was one of the few original members of the University Court present. From their opening she acted as Chairman of the Committee of the Bournville Village Schools. In 1935 she held the office of President of the Union of Educational Institutions and gave the presidential address at the fortieth annual meeting of the Union on "Education for Pleasure." Yet, with her deep concern for the right education and upbringing of the child, witnessed in the part she played in all these organizations, Elizabeth Cadbury maintained a shrewd common sense in her approach to the problem. In an address given in 1909 she stated:

> The child is considered, studied, and observed. Observation and study are essential, but . . . it may sometimes occur to us to question whether the child of to-day is not too much observed! Most good movements have their exaggerations. It may be well for the pendulum to swing back a little, and for him to experience what the parents of my generation used to call 'a little wholesome neglect.' Too much observation may produce a self-conscious and self-centred being, and may hinder him from forming a balanced appreciation of his place in the universe.[1]

Her activities for the Girls' Clubs and the Y.W.C.A. were centred in her concern for broadening and deepening the interests of the youth of her city, offering them the chance to develop gifts of self-expression in the dramatic group, the gymnasium, or the debating circle, adding to the zest of life as growing knowledge, fresh hobbies, the use of hitherto untried powers, opened up new vistas of interest and skill. To Elizabeth life was a continuing adventure, and she longed that others might find it so, might revel "in the enormous number of interesting things there were in the world with which to become acquainted." Growing years brought constant enrichment of interest, an added bloom to life as the precious hours slipped away, rather than a fading of its colours into the grey twilight of old age.

The object of education for her was to call forth within the individual the powers of virtue in the Greek sense—excellence of work, excellence in the performance of function, a quality of life which would enable its possessor to live well and to the full. If men or women were to learn to use their faculties and gifts aright, she averred, to order and rule their leisure, then first they must learn the lessons of self-discipline, must submit to the demands of intellectual and physical training, making themselves strong and active in mind and body. But the ultimate

[1] Address given to a conference of the Parents' National Education Union which met in Birmingham in 1909.

ON HER NINETIETH BIRTHDAY

The inkstand is mounted in a hoof of George Cadbury's favourite horse.

Photo H. J. Whitlock and Sons, Ltd.

A FAMILY GATHERING: MR AND MRS
EDWARD CADBURY'S GOLDEN WEDDING
DAY—OCTOBER 22, 1946

Front Row: Mrs Edward Cadbury, Mr Edward Cadbury, Dame Elizabeth Cadbury, Mr George Cadbury, Mr Henry T. Cadbury. *Second Row:* Mrs Geoffrey Hoyland (Dorothea), Mrs Bertram Crosfield (Eleanor), Mrs Kenneth Wilson (Isabel), Mr Kenneth Wilson, Mrs Laurence Cadbury, Mr Laurence Cadbury, Mrs Henry Cadbury. *Third Row:* Mr Geoffrey Hoyland, Mr Bertram Crosfield, Mr W. E. Greeves, Mrs W. E. Greeves (Marion). *Back Row:* Mr Denis Lambert, Mrs Denis Lambert (Ursula), Mr Norman Cadbury, Mrs Norman Cadbury, Mrs Egbert Cadbury, Major Egbert Cadbury.

Photo G. F. Charlton

WIND'S POINT, MALVERN

The Cadbury 'family house' for many years (formerly the home of Jenny Lind).

THE FRIENDS' MEETING HOUSE, BOURNVILLE

The portrait bust of George Cadbury is in an exterior niche of the columbarium where are deposited the ashes of many members of the Cadbury family.

purpose of it all was not a mere selfish enjoyment—it was the building of the citizen of integrity, who would battle successfully against the temptations to self-indulgence and greed, who would give himself to the service and enrichment of his community and of the human race. That was the only way to combat the growing materialism and utilitarianism which she saw infecting all classes of society. Each individual, she averred, must be led to claim his relationship with the Divine, to live his life in the light of the knowledge that comes from God.

To the needs of the young delinquent Elizabeth Cadbury was also sensitively alert. She had watched with deep interest the work of her niece, Dame Geraldine Cadbury,[1] in the establishment of Juvenile Courts for dealing with children under sixteen years of age in trouble for various reasons. But Elizabeth Cadbury pleaded that the boy or girl over sixteen and under twenty-one were only "juvenile adults," who still needed special treatment in the attempt to save them from becoming hardened criminals. In 1919 she was urging that these young people also should be tried in special courts, and that remand homes and farm colonies should be established to carry on experimental work among young delinquents who did not respond to the care and oversight of the Probation Officer, or whose home surroundings were very bad. Such changes would in no way interfere with the excellent system of placing young people on probation, but would stop their being committed to prison, which Elizabeth Cadbury deplored as an "iniquitous method" of dealing with them. When in 1926 she was made a Justice of the Peace, she remarked that her sympathies were so much with the young offender that she could seldom achieve the strictness that her fellow-members on the Bench might feel advisable.

Above all, she never lost sight of the fact that the aim of education was the unfolding of a whole personality—mental, spiritual, and physical. With her husband, she was insistent on the place that sport, physical exercise, walking and camping in the country, should hold in the life of the child and youth. In all her activities for the various youth movements of her city these needs were kept always in mind, and the possibilities for meeting them

[1] The wife of Barrow Cadbury.

explored and often made accessible by the generosity of herself and her family. She was present at the inaugural meeting of the Girls' Athletic Club at the Bournville factory in 1899, and, with her stepson Edward, rode in a bicycle gymkhana, one of the earliest events organized by that Club. She attended the meetings and sports days faithfully year by year, and at the fortieth birthday of the Club in 1939 she reviewed the change which had taken place during her lifetime in the attitude of the nation towards physical exercise for women. Although when she was a schoolgirl certain drill had been encouraged, she said, she could not imagine what would have been the result had she or any of her school-fellows appeared in shorts! But notwith-standing the restrictions of the Victorian era, she pointed out that she herself had played tennis and cricket, had learned to swim and to sail, and had even gone on walking tours with her friends, carrying a knapsack, despite the fact that "modern youth thought it had invented the walking tour which it called hiking!"

In 1909, with the opening of the Woodlands Hospital[1] for crippled children, the gift of her husband, another fresh interest came into Elizabeth Cadbury's life. Year by year the Crippled Children's Union of Birmingham had brought out to the fields of the Manor some of the little patients, 150 at a time, that they might lie on the grass and revel in country sights and sounds for a few hours. George Cadbury had longed to do more for them, and when in the early months of 1909 a house in the Bristol road, a mile or so beyond Woodbrooke, fell vacant, he purchased it for use as a hospital where the new orthopædic treatment for such children could be carried out. The hospital was officially opened on June 22; it started with thirty-seven beds, and even the stables were converted for use as a ward. In 1914 the first extensions were added and the number of beds increased to seventy. Mr Naughton Dunn was then appointed as honorary surgeon, so that henceforth cases requiring surgical treatment could be dealt with on the spot instead of being sent elsewhere. In that year also arrangements were made for the education of the children who came for periods of a year or more, and the hospital was recognized for this purpose by the

[1] Now the Royal Orthopædic Hospital. (See p. 144.)

Board of Education. Elizabeth was most deeply interested in this development; she acted as Chairman of the House Committee from its inception, until the hospital was taken over by the State in 1948, and was chairman of the education committee of the hospital under the new scheme. Throughout the greater part of her life she visited the Woodlands almost daily, watching the progress of the children in their school tasks and handicrafts, delighting with them in their little achievements, and strengthening them in the battle to overcome physical handicaps.

In her concern to make life as happy as possible for the children who must pass perhaps months or years under treatment at the Woodlands, Elizabeth Cadbury showed both imagination and humour. On her daily visits she would take her two small dogs, whose gambols and tricks were a never-failing source of amusement; she lured the manager of a near-by circus to send his camel over, and it was led among the beds of the children lying out of doors—slow, ungainly, disdainful, looking over the heads of the delighted audience with its usual supercilious sneer. Sometimes it would be a pony provided by Arnold Edmundson, organizer of the Bournville Youths' Club, who came nuzzling the pillows in search of biscuits or sugar, and on whose back the more agile could ride; or it might be a jazz-band, organized by the Youths' and Girls' Clubs among the little patients themselves, the instruments played lustily by the bedridden, including a small piper with spinal trouble who must lie prone with his head at a lower level than his body! Elizabeth Cadbury found that the children could enjoy themselves acting from their beds, giving added verve and emphasis to the dialogue —skilful at depicting a mood merely by change of expression or the slightest gesture. In such ways she helped them to discover for themselves a fuller life of their own.

In these years, also, a greater opportunity of providing holidays for children from the slum quarters of Birmingham was made possible by the building of a house, the Beeches, for this purpose in 1908. Several years before, in 1895, George and Elizabeth Cadbury, with the vivid realization of the crowded, dreary homes in which many of their adult-school members lived, decided that they would buy a house near Bournville to which the children at least could be invited to spend their holidays in happy and healthy surroundings. During the summer months, with the aid of members of the Women's Class at Severn Street, they were enabled to lodge and entertain relays of children, thirty at a time. "Two splendid people were appointed to help with this fascinating plan," wrote Elizabeth of the scheme.

The children called them 'Father and Mother Cole' and learned to love them devotedly.

On the evening of arrival each child was weighed and bathed, and if necessary given new clothes (in the early years of this venture Mrs Cole sometimes found that children had been sewn in for the winter—that is, they never had their clothes removed).

Mr and Mrs Cole found also that most of the children had been used to being given 'a piece' when running in from school, and taking it into the streets to eat it. For the first day or two the children were not very hungry, but after settling down, appetites became huge and plate after plate of good things disappeared. This, with the fresh air, and regular sleep brought about almost incredible improvement in health and in addition to weight. It was a great joy to welcome the children to tea at the Manor once a fortnight. Mr and Mrs Cole had a beautiful collie dog called Bob and an interesting grey parrot, and the children, almost without knowing it, absorbed lessons of kindness to animals.

So the children returned to their homes, not only well and vigorous, but with the experience of a real home life and of wholesome fun in beautiful surroundings.

During the winter women officers from the Salvation Army were invited for a holiday to the Beeches and to enjoy a period of rest. "This branch of the work was very near to the heart of my husband," Elizabeth tells us. Both husband and wife had a deep admiration for the work of General Booth's new and vigorous body among the slum population and the outcasts of society, and both were deeply influenced by its example.

The new house, especially built for the purpose of a holiday home with its greater possibilities for usefulness, was another source of interest and concern to Elizabeth Cadbury. Her care for the amusement and the rebuilding of both body and mind of the children and adults who found sanctuary there was another constant claim upon her time and her imagination.[1]

II

No woman as active and alert as Elizabeth Cadbury could stand aloof from the strange and bitter contest which was being fought out in these years between the sexes, as women struggled to win for themselves the right to vote. She had long been concerned that women should recognize their need to submit to the discipline of intellectual training. More and more she saw that they were being called upon to make decisions which required a wide knowledge of facts and demanded a clear judgment and the power to make such decisions impersonally. For unnumbered generations, she said, the emotional rather than the intellectual side of the average woman had been developed and exercised; what was now needed was a training of the mind that would lead to more thought and less feeling. But, while realizing this weakness in her contemporaries, Elizabeth was clear that women should have a voice in the affairs of the nation, and played her part, albeit a small one, as a steadying influence among the storms of outraged passion.

In the course of her life she had seen the members of her own sex struggling to gain a new status in society, and slowly winning their way, step by step, into the closed citadels of higher education and the professions. A traveller in the year 1870, passing through the City of London, would not have found a woman employed in any of the humming offices or warehouses; he would scarcely have caught the flicker of a skirt or gown among

[1] The Beeches was put to varied uses in the testing times that lay ahead. From 1914–18 it became a war hospital, in which Elizabeth Cadbury's daughter Dorothea was one of the nurses. For a time it housed the girls' classes of the Day Continuation Schools. In the long years of depression and unemployment between the two World Wars, at the suggestion of the National Council for Social Service, it was used as a residential training centre for unemployed women from all parts of the country who were members of National Service Clubs. In the Second World War it housed the staff and students of the Working Women's College, evacuated from Surbiton. After their return it was used for a time as a hostel for students attending Birmingham University. It was subsequently taken over by Cadbury Brothers Limited as a residential institution for training people in the grocery and confectionery trades.

the ranks of the frock-coats thronging the pavements. By 1900
the invasion of commercial offices and the Civil Service by
women clerks was complete, an accomplished, accepted, and
unnoticed fact. But, although women were beginning to play
an increasingly active role in the social and commercial life of the
country, no political party was prepared to grant them the vote
or to make the question of their enfranchisement an election
issue. Thus women themselves, in the early years of the century,
formed their own movements to wage the campaign—first,
the quieter Women's Suffrage Society, working by constitutional
means; secondly, the militant Women's Social and Political Union
under the leadership of Sylvia and Christabel Pankhurst.

With the actions of the militant suffragettes Elizabeth had no
sympathy and constantly expressed her regret that they continued their tactics. But she was in close accord with the
constitutional suffragist movement and a keen advocate of the
right of women to vote and to enter Parliament. When, early
in 1912, it appeared that a Conciliation Bill, in which all schools
of suffragist thought were united, had a very good chance of
passing its third reading in the House of Commons, her hopes
for a final settlement of the problem were high. "Everyone
looked forward to the discussion in the House on Thursday,"
she wrote on April 6 of that year, after attending a suffrage
meeting in Birmingham. "I think everyone expected the Conciliation Bill to be passed, and it was a bitter disappointment to the
workers when on Friday we heard that the majority was against
it. It is very feeble that the members should be influenced by the
outrageous conduct of a few fanatics, which shows that men are
not really logical as this does not alter the principle involved."

III

Behind all this growing round of activities were the constant
claims of family life. Her older stepchildren were marrying and
setting out to found homes and families of their own,[1] and amid

[1] Edward Cadbury was married to Dorothy Howitt in 1896, George
Cadbury to Edith Woodall in 1902; Eleanor, the younger stepdaughter, was
married to Bertram Crosfield in April 1910, Isabel, the elder, to Kenneth
Wilson in 1911, and Henry, the youngest stepson, to Lucy Bellows, of
Gloucester, in 1912.

all her other duties were the arrangements for the successive weddings, and the plans for the new homes and their staffing, all of which Elizabeth Cadbury took in her stride. Dorothea was seriously ill in the spring of 1906, undergoing the then rare operation for appendicitis, and her mother did not leave her bedside till the danger was past. In September 1908 Elizabeth's greatly loved sister, Janet, died at the Manor House after a long and painful illness. It was during these weeks of strain and tension that the *Standard*, a London daily paper no longer in existence, launched an attack on Cadbury Brothers for their alleged indifference to the slave conditions under which was produced the cocoa they purchased—the attack which led to the famous libel action of 1909. Through it all Elizabeth went on her way, outwardly calm and undaunted, whatever were the inner pangs of loss and of bitterness.

She could rise to any occasion, from an outbreak of German measles in the household almost on the eve of Eleanor's wedding, when the two hundred guests had to be notified at once lest any feared to come, to the delicate task of winning the friendship and confidence of her new sons- and daughters-in-law, and bringing them a sense of belonging to her close-knit family circle. "She never interfered, but she was always there if one wanted help or advice," was the spontaneous testimony of the wife of one of her sons, echoed, in slightly different phraseology, by all the newcomers to her family. And there followed the interest and delight of a growing number of grandchildren to welcome and learn to know as fresh and vivid personalities.

The Edwardian years, before the disruption of the old order by the first world conflict, were busy times, too, for Elizabeth, in a wider sphere of social relationships than those of the growing family circle or her colleagues on committees and councils. She was eager that her children should have the chance of a full social life in their young manhood and womanhood, and she herself moved in circles which many members of the Society of Friends had neither the opportunity nor the inclination to enter. George Cadbury would seldom dine out, but his wife had no such inhibitions. She would sometimes go to dinner parties alone, or she would carry off her older stepsons and

-daughters to a Lord Mayor's reception in Birmingham, to the Bishop of Birmingham's garden party, or to the Prime Minister's reception at the Foreign Office among the glittering uniforms and orders. She and her husband frequently attended the Royal Garden Party, travelling down by special train to Windsor or driving in a carriage up the Mall to Buckingham Palace. Every year Elizabeth herself gave a garden party at the Manor, to which two or three hundred people were invited; by 1910 she had so far broken with the Puritanical tradition of her upbringing that the guests at a New Year's party at her home were called upon to dance. In any circle of society in which she moved she could hold her own, because always she had the gift of meeting men and women as individuals, and for the moment the person she encountered really held the centre of her interest, and would respond to a frank, direct approach which broke down barriers of reserve and stiffness and pierced to the essential person beneath. Elizabeth enjoyed all her social contacts, but it was finally the human being and his worth as such in whose friendship she found satisfaction. A title might add glamour, but if there was no character behind it she quickly lost interest.

It was at this time that Percy Bigland, the Quaker artist, painted her portrait (1908). It reveals a woman, glowing with health in middle age, strong to the point of domination, not lightly to be crossed, but with lines of humour that suggest the capacity to laugh at herself as well as at others, direct, courageous, a little overwhelming on first acquaintance. It is the portrait of one who may develop with the passing years in either of two directions, to a self-willed, self-opinionated, and difficult old age, harsh in its judgments, or to a ripening and deepening of character, a smoothing-down of the incipient hardness that might result in unsuspected gentleness.

At the end of January in the year 1913 Elizabeth Cadbury was suddenly faced with one of the most testing challenges to her courage. It was a particularly sunny, clear, and frosty day, and her husband left the house in good spirits and apparently in his usual health to walk as usual to the factory. Within a few hours his wife was suddenly summoned by her son Norman to go over to the factory where George had been taken ill. When

Elizabeth entered his office she found him lying unconscious on a sofa and learned that he had collapsed and passed into a coma while dictating letters to his secretary. Sir Robert Simon was hurriedly called from Birmingham, and on his arrival took a very serious view of the condition of the patient. It was agreed to try to get him home. "I cannot tell you what an experience it was bringing him in the ambulance and carrying him upstairs to his room, quite unconscious, after seeing him start out so brightly a few hours previously," wrote Elizabeth to her children. She telegraphed for Sir Thomas Barlow from London, determined to spare no effort to save her husband, though it was obvious that Sir Robert Simon did not expect him to regain consciousness. When the latter, who had to go out on another call, returned about five he was astonished to find that George was slowly reviving and had already spoken to his wife. By eight-thirty, when Sir Thomas Barlow arrived, and the doctors held a consultation, he could answer their questions quite clearly. "They both describe it as little short of a miracle—in fact Sir Robert Simon said he had never had a similar experience," wrote the anxious wife and mother to her family. Eventually George made a good recovery, though he had to lead a rather less active life in future; within a week he was well enough for his wife to leave him for a few hours to give a lecture on Public Health to a Manchester Society in the Town Hall of that city, and by the middle of February she was able to carry him off to Bordighera to gain strength in the Mediterranean sunshine. But for the first few days Elizabeth looked with dread into the Valley of the Shadow and the bitter pain of a final parting; in the coming years there must always have been the fear, hidden in the background, that once again the blow might fall with the same cruel suddenness, this time finally to sever the thread of life.

10

The Years of the First World War

In May 1914 Elizabeth was in Rome with her daughters Dorothea (Dollie) and Mollie, attending a meeting of the International Council of Women, where she was elected Convenor of the Peace Committee. Her brother Wilfrid had died in South Africa the preceding Christmas, and on her return to the Manor his widow and her little son Knox were much at the house, as they had come to make their home in Birmingham. Towards the end of July came news of the passing of yet another member of her family, her sister Frances, who was a missionary in West Africa, so that the weeks preceding the outbreak of the first great war were shadowed by these losses of her childhood companions.

Then, suddenly, in the closing days of July the telegraph wires were humming with demands and mobilization orders; troop trains and bodies of marching men crowded the rails and the roads to the frontiers of Germany, Austria, France, and Russia, and England found herself unbelievably on the brink of war. Elizabeth Cadbury was caught up in the last-minute efforts to hold back her country from the plunge into the abyss. "Creeping shadows of war—telegrams flying to Asquith and Sir Edward Grey on behalf of the Peace Committee of the International Women's Council urging neutrality—hopes and fears about war—Germany in Belgium—continuous wires and messages as to progress of negotiations." So run the hurried notes in her diary from July 31 to August 3, when she and George Cadbury were spending a few days at Wind's Point. On Tuesday, August 4, she went to London to speak at a meeting organized by the National Council of Women in the Kingsway Hall, taking her place on the platform beside Mrs Fawcett, Mrs Creighton, Mrs Swanwick, and a number of foreigners. Afterwards she walked through the streets where the excited crowds thronged Whitehall, and pressed against the railings of Buckingham Palace.

"War declared last night. Black outlook. All shops deserted—general gloom," is the entry for August 5. The war was to break into her family life within a few days. At the end of the week Egbert arrived very late at the Manor to say that his friends the Garnetts were offering their yacht to the Admiralty for minesweeping or hospital work, and he, with a group of other Cambridge undergraduates, wished to join the enterprise. A few days later he was off to Brightlingsea to join the crew. In 1915 he was seconded to the Royal Naval Air Service, and in the closing years of the war brought down the last zeppelin to cross the English coast. For his services he was awarded the D.F.C. and D.S.O. By the early autumn of 1914 Laurence had joined a camp of young men Friends at Jordans, in Buckinghamshire, who were training in ambulance work, the beginning of the Friends' Ambulance Unit, and on October 21 he left for France. He quickly rose to the position of organizer of transport of the F.A.U. in Flanders, operating immediately behind the French lines. He not only helped with the wounded, but rescued many French peasants from the on-rolling German armies, and was awarded the Croix de Guerre for his services. Mollie, early in September, arranged to take a course of nursing at the Queen's Hospital; she later volunteered to go as a nurse with the Friends' Ambulance Unit, and for two years was nursing in various hospitals close to the field of battle. Norman, the engineer of the family, turned his works over to the fulfilment of War Office and Admiralty orders. His days were long and strenuous, and it became a family custom to migrate to the kitchen, where his food had been kept hot, and spend the last hours of the day talking with him round the dying embers of the kitchen fire and sharing all the family news.

Dorothea trained as a V.A.D. and nursed the wounded in the military hospital which took over the Beeches. Later she also served on the land. Thus, as in many Quaker homes in both world wars, Elizabeth found that the members of her family were divided as to where their allegiance lay, and to each she left complete freedom of choice in following the diverse claims of conscience.

Having watched the battle within her own family circle to discover the particular service to which each member felt himself or herself called, Elizabeth, for all her work for peace, was not prepared to take up a doctrinaire pacifist position.

The Society of Friends as a whole remained steadily entrenched behind its historic peace testimony. But many Friends like herself found themselves grappling with doubts and questionings to which there was no easy answer. A large number of the strong and active younger members, both men and women, were not content to stand aside in that dark hour of peril and suffering, and so they formed the voluntary societies of the Friends' Ambulance Unit and the Friends' War Victims Relief Committee, both of which were at work in France and Flanders by the winter of 1914. Between two and three hundred young men of the Society were serving with the Army and Navy by May 1915, and the Monthly Meetings were urging London Yearly Meeting to take no steps with regard to their disownment at least until the conflict had been ended for some time, and the first emotional storms had quietened.

For the man or woman who believed that their testimony against war could be given only by a complete refusal to have any part or lot with the State in arms, rejecting both ambulance or relief work or any form of non-combatant service, and willing to suffer imprisonment and death if need be at the dictate of conscience, Elizabeth had a respect but little understanding. Could the threat of violence, the demoralization and brutality of a State drunk with power be met by a negative and a withdrawal from the claims of the community? Had not the pacifist yet to discover the constructive and dynamic counter-challenge, the effective and positive answer to these evils?

With such thoughts in mind, Elizabeth went up to attend the adjourned Yearly Meeting of the Society of Friends, held in January 1916, when the British Government first introduced military conscription. It was called to consider the position of the young men of military age in the Society of Friends, and to give them an opportunity of deciding on their course of action. "The big Meeting House was packed," she writes in her journal letters. "There were a great number of men who had apparently not attended a Yearly Meeting before; there was a great sense of vigorous life and purpose; there were many Friends present with high ideals and deep spiritual experience, but after all, one is inclined to ask, were the meetings really meetings of the Society of Friends, or of a new Society, building on our past, adopting many of our principles, but not the Society we know and value? The over-emphasis of one of our tenets, one that means so much at the present time, seems to have overshadowed other principles, equally dear, and even more fundamental to many of the Society." She pointed out that the inclusion of a 'conscience' clause in the Military Service Act was the acknowledgment by the Government of the possibility of a higher claim than its own on the allegiance of the British subject, and this she felt in itself distinguished a different attitude on the part of the politicians never hitherto found in any previous conflict. She therefore found it difficult to accept the refusal of non-combatant service by the able-bodied young men of the Society in the name of Quakerism, and made her position abundantly clear, incurring unpopularity in Quaker circles thereby.

The great issues that would emerge from the chaos of the War years were never forgotten or minimized by her. In June 1914 a new body, the Peace and International Relations Committee, had been formed by the National Council of Women, of which Elizabeth was made the first Convener, or chairman. This Committee met first in October 1914, when war had already been raging for two months. Under Elizabeth Cadbury's guidance as chairman, it did what was possible during the four years of conflict to promote an intelligent public opinion, a right judgment, and an atmosphere of goodwill in face of the growing bitterness against Germany. A number of informative public lectures were given, interest was taken in aliens interned in Britain, contact was maintained so far as was possible with branches of the National Councils of Women in other countries, mobilizing their forces to do what they could to mitigate the suffering of war and invasion. Throughout, in the meetings of

Committee and Council, Elizabeth maintained the right of the pacifist to follow the claims of his conscience, and gained much criticism thereby from some of her colleagues in the movement. One irate lady, leaving a meeting of the Council, denounced its Peace Committee as a pro-German organization, and obviously placed its chairman among those she deemed 'arch-traitors'! But Elizabeth's high integrity, her loyalty to principle, made a deep impression on those who worked closely with her in these gatherings.

She found a practical outlet for her desire to serve in her work for the refugees from a war-torn Europe who came flocking into Birmingham. The first fifty Belgians arrived early in September of 1914, and thereafter came in a steady stream till by January 1 of the following year some 2500 had found a home in that city.[1] Elizabeth was from the outset a member of the Executive Committee, which planned for the care of these strangers, and became Chairman of what she described as "a marvellous and wise Committee," the Allocation Committee, which interviewed each family on arrival, discovered their special needs, investigated relationships with other refugees, and found a suitable home for the newcomers. The Committee included among its members Norman Birkett (later Lord Justice Birkett), the Rev. Arnold Pinchard, Mrs Gerald Feeny, Evelyn Sturge, and Miss Eveleen Downes, who acted as Secretary. A house was taken at No. 44 Islington Row, on September 4, 1914, as a temporary centre and hostel, where the refugees could first be sorted out, and a band of voluntary helpers was enlisted. The incomers were passed on from here as quickly as possible to the various homes arranged for them by the Allocation Committee.

A first report of the Committee recalls vividly to mind the difficulties of large-scale evacuation experienced by a later generation in 1939.

> The memory of those early days is composed of train loads of refugees sent without warning, for whom accommodation had to be found on the instant; train loads of refugees who did not arrive

---

[1] In all, Birmingham received, housed, and cared for some 5000 Belgian refugees.

when accommodation and hospitality had been most carefully prepared; of bands of workers who patrolled the station platforms looking for the trains, which, despite the advice of the London Committee, never arrived; of trains which did arrive when no band of workers was there at all; of demands made late at night upon Institutions to provide meals and accommodation; of explanations to the Institutions when this had been done and the accommodation was not required; and above all a memory of 44 Islington Row, crowded to overflowing with refugees of all kinds —men, women and children—with their pitiful little bundles, representing all their worldly goods.

In many towns and cities the unfortunate strangers created serious problems, but in Birmingham, due to the careful arrangements made by the Executive and its sub-committees, the majority of the Belgian guests soon settled down quietly among the English citizens, earning their own livings, saving their money with astonishing thrift for the day of their return home, and contributing regularly and generously towards the maintenance of their fellow-countrymen who were left in dire straits in Belgium. Mr Walter Long, who was then President of the Local Government Board, expressed his particular appreciation of the assistance rendered by the Birmingham Committee, in conjunction with the Trade Unions, by placing Belgians in useful industrial employment and thus helping to make them happy and contented.

Even more dramatic than the great influx of the Belgians was the arrival in Birmingham of a group of twenty-five Serbian boys, after a journey of hazardous adventure and extreme hardship. These youths, the eldest of whom was seventeen and the youngest nine, the sons of peasants, fled from their homes before the advancing Austrian army, and attached themselves to straggling companies of Serbians during the retreat. They were often on the verge of starvation, plodding on wearily mile after mile on the long trek to the Adriatic coast. One, aged eleven, who fell in with a Serbian mountain battery in the retreat to Albania, was given a uniform by the soldiers and dubbed "The General," a title of which he was very proud. He was present in some desperate encounters with the Bulgarians, and through weeks of great hardship pressed onwards by stony mountain tracks and through the shadows of great forests, till he reached the Adriatic. Here the boys were succoured by the French military authorities and were eventually sent to England in company with other young refugees, three hundred in all.

A committee was formed in Birmingham to deal with the contingent of twenty-five sent to that city, and of this Elizabeth was also chairman. The boys were sent to the Bournville Village Schools and the Kings Norton Secondary School for their education, and a home was made for them in a house in Selly Oak, lent to the Committee by Mrs Alfred Wiggin, of Bordesley Hall. It was the first hostel for Serbians opened in the country, and here the boys were able to live a healthy, active life, with plenty of outlet for their young energies in the carpenter's or metal-working shops, in playing games in the garden, or in being initiated into the lore of Scouting, whereby responsibility for the well-being and discipline of the hostel was thrown largely on the older boys.

For her services to these young Serbians Elizabeth, with three other helpers, was given the Serbian Red Cross of Honour at the end of the war. Many years later, when attending a meeting of the International Council of Women in Dubrovnik, she motored on to Belgrade and met again twelve of the boys, grown into manhood and all holding responsible positions in their own country. The education and the happy life provided by the citizens of Birmingham had borne sound fruit.

Shortly after the war, in 1922, when Austria, truncated and starving, was in a desperate plight, fifteen Austrian children were invited to come for a time and live in homes at Bournville where new sources of strength and of happiness could be built up for the future. Elizabeth and other members of her family were at Bournville to welcome the children on their arrival and to talk to them in their own language. A few days later Elizabeth presented each child with a dictionary which she had purchased especially for them from various booksellers in the city. The children quickly learned English and rejoiced in the home and school life and the care of their foster-parents. George Cadbury each week would make a round of the homes where they were staying, his pockets full of chocolate, and watched with delight the thin, pale faces growing plump and rosy, as the children responded to good nourishment and fresh air and forgot the dark privations of the past.

Throughout the years of war difficulties of transport, when petrol for private use was severely curtailed, in no wise hampered Elizabeth's activities or her regular attendance at committees. Through rain and snow and slush or the summer heat she walked or bicycled, or sometimes drove in a pony-trap, and remarked with surprise and pleasure how few people allowed the difficulties to interrupt their round of voluntary work for the community. Between her committees she would spend a few hours vigorously gardening, trying to keep the grounds in order with her greatly depleted staff. And still, amid the black-out and the difficulties of war-time travel, she would hurry off by bus and train to attend a concert in Birmingham at the end of a day's duties, which in themselves would have worn out a less strong and vigorous woman.

Fresh projects took shape; a hostel organized by the Y.W.C.A. for girls who came thronging into Birmingham to make munitions; plans for nursery schools under the Fisher Act of 1918; the starting of Child Welfare Clinics, and a clinic for remedial exercises for school children, a scheme which Elizabeth Cadbury pushed with energy. One of her daughters had suffered as a child from curvature of the spine, and she had seen the great difference to the girl's health which skilled and expert care and exercise had produced, and characteristically desired that all children suffering from such troubles should have the same advantages.

She was an active member of a new Anglo-Russian Society, formed to promote a greater understanding between the two countries, and in 1916 was elected to the National Peace Council. This was a body first formed in 1908 as a federation of various national societies which were concerned directly or indirectly in the promotion of peace and the development of international goodwill and co-operation. Its distinctive purpose is to encourage common action in support of a radical and constructive solution of the problem of war. From 1924 till 1946 Elizabeth Cadbury

I

acted as Treasurer of the Council and on her retirement was made a Vice-President, an office which she held till her death.

The membership included every range of pacifist opinion, shading from the empirical approach of the politician with his eye constantly upon the electorate, through the chill individualism of the intellectual prepared to oppose to the claims of government a rational and responsible disobedience, to the unyielding faith of the ideologist, lit by the fires of fanaticism, whose pacifism is his sole religion.

Meetings were sometimes stormy, and Elizabeth's good sense and ready humour were often a saving factor in the situation. "There are few people more cantankerous than pacifists," she remarked once as she walked away with the secretary from a particularly difficult session. But the catholicity of her own outlook enabled her to appreciate and weigh fairly the contribution that the different sections of opinion had to offer. When the question of the appointment of a new secretary arose in 1930, and her own nominee was finally not selected, to her great disappointment, the newcomer who was chosen found to his surprise that the strong-willed woman who had opposed his election was prepared to offer him the most loyal service and support, and a warm friendship grew up between them. She would fight to the last for the realization of her own wishes, but when these were overruled by the concensus of opinion in a meeting she not only gave way with good grace, but, as in this instance, would throw her energies into furthering the desires of the group that ran counter to her own. Her standards of loyalty to her friends, to the causes she served, to her vision of truth, were high, and in that greater loyalty she could forget and resolve her own immediate sense of disappointment or frustration.

Two more of her family were married in the course of the war years, Egbert to Mary Forbes Phillips, the daughter of a clergyman, and herself a professional singer who often appeared on the concert platform and operatic stage, and Mollie[1] to William Greeves, a young Northern Irishman serving with the Friends' Ambulance Unit. The difficulties of carrying through a war-time wedding with the limitations of rationing Elizabeth

[1] Now Senator and M.B.E.

tackled with a cheerful aplomb. In October 1918, a few months after Mollie's marriage, the whole Cadbury household was stricken with the prevailing scourge of influenza, nine members falling ill at once. Those who were left well and active spent the time in housework and nursing, "which we thoroughly enjoy," stated Elizabeth, treating the whole trying situation with her customary light-heartedness. Then, early in November, Dorothea succumbed; pneumonia rapidly developed, and for several days her life hung in the balance. The joke had changed overnight into a grim struggle for life. "The Proclamation of Peace, the abdication of the Emperor, and the convulsions in Europe have passed us by almost like a dream," wrote Elizabeth Cadbury on November 13, when the crisis was past and at last there was hope of her daughter's recovery. "I have heard distant guns, and on Tuesday afternoon the sound of the Bournville bells came in at the window as I sat by Dollie, but it has been curious to have been entirely cut off from the outer world when such wonderful things were happening. Twelve years ago, a day or two after Dollie's operation, when again we wondered whether she was to be taken from us, the celebrations of Chamberlain's seventieth birthday took place, and that evening the sounds from the city and its surroundings penetrated more shrilly the walls of the house than did the murmur of the armistice rejoicings."

So, from the shadow of death, sobered by the experience of those anxious weeks of watching, but with undaunted courage, she turned to face the challenge of the new and different world emerging from the chaos of war.

11

New Civic and Political Ventures

WHEN the Congress of Versailles began its sittings to discuss the terms of the Peace Treaty Elizabeth Cadbury hurried off to Paris, together with Lady Aberdeen, Mrs Fawcett, and Mrs Corbett Ashby, taking her stepson Henry with her. The little group of English women, with the addition of a few others, held a conference with the leaders of the Congress, to press for the inclusion of women in the ranks of the peacemakers. They were given a kind reception, and, whether as a result of these talks or not they hardly knew, but more than one woman was given a place on the Council of the League of Nations, and later Elizabeth Cadbury noticed when attending the League Assembly at Geneva that these women had been accorded full membership of the Council.

When the League of Nations Union was formed she became a most active member, and a leader in the local branch in her district of Birmingham. Year by year she was present in Geneva when the Assembly of the League met, following the discussions, particularly those which centred on the question of disarmament, with the most alert attention. Her regular attendance at the Assembly enabled her to keep the members of her Midland city alive to the great questions of the moment and able to follow them with intelligence. It was her practice also to include younger members of her family and their friends in her party each year at Geneva, including her grandchildren as they grew old enough, so that the rising generation might gain some insight into the movements of world opinion, and might be fitted to play an informed and responsible part in their own circles in the effort for a better international understanding.

In the autumn of 1919 Elizabeth broke entirely new ground by entering for the first time the field of local politics. She accepted nomination for the Birmingham City Council at a by-election which occurred in the Kings Norton Ward. It was the period of the immediate post-war boom, when wages and prices were soaring, and expenditure both public and private was on a lavish scale as compared with pre-1914 standards. The newly created Ministry of Health had launched the first scheme for house-building by local authorities which was to be aided by a national grant. Efforts for improving educational standards and facilities were envisaged in the Fisher Act of 1918. The Sankey Commission had just been appointed, and had begun its inquiry into the coal industry—that Royal Commission which was to report in the spring of 1920 that "the present system of ownership and working stands condemned." The Russian revolution had acted as a spur both to intellectuals and to workers in Britain, urging them ahead into the dimly seen, opening vistas of an illimitable future. Was it surprising that many felt that they stood on the threshold of a new era of social justice, of greater economic equality, of "good times for all"?

It was in this atmosphere of unrest, of large and vague hopes, of the beginning of an incipient struggle between the Trade Unions and the older forces of parliamentary government for control of the State, that Elizabeth accepted her candidature for the municipal election. She stood as a progressive independent. Her programme included support for Fisher's Education Act as providing greater equality of opportunity for all classes, the improvement and extension of the school health service, a practical interest in housing reform and warm support of municipal action in providing houses, and the provision of playing fields and open spaces in every neighbourhood.

At first it was thought that Elizabeth would be returned unopposed, but the Labour Party finally put up a woman candidate of their own. After a strenuous electioneering campaign Elizabeth topped the poll by nearly a thousand votes.

On December 1 she wrote:

The past ten days, on looking back, seem like a dream. If events had culminated differently on Saturday I should say like a horrible nightmare, but as it turned out, I shall, after a short time, remember only the extraordinary kindness, loyalty and trust which I found

in a hundred unexpected quarters. This being my first experience
of the working of an election, I have considerably added to my
knowledge of life and of human nature.

The new office brought an increased burden of duties which
were faithfully carried out during her four years as a member of
the Council. Though she did not stand again for election,
Elizabeth was always proud of the fact that she had been able
to serve England's second city in this capacity.

Fresh interests were also brought by the marriage of her
daughter Dorothea to Geoffrey Hoyland in the summer of 1919.
He was the stepson of Elizabeth's sister Josephine, and was head-
master of the boys' preparatory school known as The Downs,
at Colwall, in the Malvern Hills. Henceforth Elizabeth Cadbury
followed the development and activities of the school with close
attention; many of her grandsons were pupils there, and a great
summer party for the boys was always held at Wind's Point
at the season of strawberries and ice-cream.

In May 1919 came the visit of George V and Queen Mary to
the village of Bournville and the Works, when Elizabeth Cadbury
walked with her husband and the royal visitors on their tour of
inspection. She had already met Queen Mary on several occasions,
and found that the Queen shared many of her interests; the visit
to Bournville forged a new link of sympathy and understanding.

So the years slipped by, each more busy than the last, years
always to be precious in memory because they were the last that
Elizabeth Cadbury spent with her husband.

By January 1922 it became obvious that George Cadbury
was failing in health. For the following months he had to spend
most of the time resting on a couch or in bed, with the occasional
change of a motor drive through the country. His wife would
slip away from her place beside his couch to attend her multifarious committees, to visit those in sickness or distress, or to
pay a flying call on her married children, hurrying back to him
the moment that she could. As the days passed it became clear
that this time there was to be no lifting of the shadow, and
quietly and courageously the husband and wife prepared themselves for the end and for the long parting after thirty-four years

of married fellowship and close co-operation in work and plans. George Cadbury appeared to be somewhat stronger in the autumn, and was able once again to spend a little time at the Bournville Works in October, but on the 20th of that month new symptoms developed, and he passed into unconsciousness. "The last days of my husband's life were very peaceful," Elizabeth Cadbury wrote twenty years later. "On 24th October he had been resting very quietly in his room; I was sitting beside him and his faithful physician standing by. The windows were open; it was five o'clock, and across the fields came the Bournville signal for home-going; a few minutes later the doctor murmured, 'He, too, has gone home.'" Four days later, on October 28, a memorial service was held, "not in a church or hall, but on the village green at Bournville, where thousands of his friends gathered together to pay their last tribute of affection and farewell."

Elizabeth Cadbury was thus left at the age of sixty-four, the head of her large family, and with the responsibility of carrying on certain of her husband's interests in addition to her own. A first task which she assumed on his death was the Chairmanship of the Bournville Village Trust. One who knew her well throughout her married life stated that he felt her work in this capacity was among her greatest achievements, in which her ability and administrative gifts were proved to the utmost and came triumphantly through the test.

The work of the Trust had increased considerably since the building of the original village. George Cadbury in the Trust Deed had inserted certain clauses which gave the Trustees freedom to try new experiments as the passing years brought fresh needs. Five Public Utility Societies are now working on the Bournville Estate. The first was formed as early as 1907; the second, in 1914, developed the Weoley Hill Estate of nearly five hundred houses as a residential suburb; the third, established in 1919, was confined to the workers in the factory. Two further Societies were set up under Elizabeth's chairmanship—the Woodlands Housing Society, and the company known as Residential Flats Limited. She took a great interest in St George's Court, a block of flats for business and professional women, built by this latter body, and in later years in Brook House, a terrace of maisonettes, built by Copec on Bournville land, and also designed for women living alone.

Many experiments have been tried by the Trust in providing dwellings to meet the needs of special classes of people, such as the newly married and the elderly; in the use of different types of building material and house equipment; in financing housing schemes at Bournville and elsewhere; in initiating research into problems of town-planning and the relation of town and country-side; and later in 'self-build' enterprises.

Bournville itself has never been a 'company' village attached to the Cadbury factory. The proportion of those living on the estate who are the employees of Cadbury Brothers has remained fairly constant, at about 40 per cent. Since 1911 the village has been included as a suburb of the Greater Birmingham and is not self-contained. Nevertheless it does enjoy many physical and social attractions which are not commonly provided either by municipal or commercial landowners.

The Estate has grown from the 338 acres with some 300 houses which George Cadbury handed over to the Trust in 1900, to over 1000 acres with about 3000 houses and a population of over 9000 people. Since 1935 it has joined with the city of Birmingham and the National Trust in efforts to preserve a belt of agricultural land on the outskirts of the city to prevent this being entirely submerged in the outward sprawl of urban houses. The Bournville Village Trust owns 1606 acres of such land and manages for the National Trust another 456 acres. These estates are maintained as farmland, but parts are accessible to the town dwellers for rambles and camping, for picnics and week-end excursions; in the 'green belt' the walker, the camper, and the tired mother from the gloomy streets of the city can find new pleasures and recreation.[1]

[1] The Bournville Village Trust has also lent its architects to Copec to carry out rehabilitation work in the slums of Birmingham. The Copec House Improvement Society Limited was a practical outcome of the Copec (Conference on Politics, Economics and Citizenship) conference held by the Churches in Birmingham soon after the First World War. A recent Copec development at Bournville has been the erection of a block of flats for elderly people of some means who are in need of nursing care and attention.

The monthly meetings of the twelve Trustees have always a long agenda, ranging from new plans for building or some special project of research into housing conditions and the future growth of Birmingham to the plea of a small cricket club for the lease of a pitch on land controlled by the Trust. For twenty-nine years upon Elizabeth Cadbury as chairman rested the responsibility to guide and stimulate such discussions and plans. She would enter into details with unsparing energy; a typical entry in her diary occurs on September 24, 1923: "Miss Stuart and I were over at the Estate office and flats [St George's Court] on Tuesday. We found that the electric supply people had said they doubted being able to have the current in the flats for another month, so in the afternoon I called on the Chief Engineer, with the result that he has promised that it shall be ready about the middle of this week."

While her chief personal interest lay in the 'old' village and its people, she was ready to enter fully into the fresh projects and ideas put forward by her fellow Trustees, eager to grasp the opportunities that changing conditions opened before them.

On her own account she was still ready at the age of sixty-five to launch out anew in the stormy sea of national politics. In 1923, the year following her husband's death, Elizabeth accepted the Liberal Party's invitation to stand for Parliament as their candidate in the autumn election.

The exhilaration and eager anticipations of the immediate post-war period had died away in frustration and disappointment. Unemployment was growing, exports were shrinking, agricultural prices were falling calamitously, the demand for industrial capital had shrunk away. By June 1921, 2,580,000 people were without work. Men and women were sickened by the brutalities of the Black-and-Tan régime and the Irish Civil War. At the end of 1922, when Germany defaulted on her reparation payments, France marched into the Ruhr, and the bitter campaign of passive resistance began, to end in the chaos of inflation. In the spring of 1923 Bonar Law died, and Baldwin, then a little-known figure, was called to succeed him as Premier. The Conservatives, under Bonar Law, had taken office in the autumn of 1922 under the electoral pledge that they would not introduce any protective tariff; Baldwin believed, on the other hand, that the tariff was the only possible means of attempting to deal with the problem of unemployment. Therefore he felt bound to dissolve Parliament, and in the autumn of 1923 he went to the country on the issue of tariff reform. The Asquithian and Lloyd Georgian Liberals united in their opposition to this proposal, as the Party had united, after its differences over the Boer War, to combat Joseph Chamberlain's tariff-reform measures a generation earlier.

This was the situation into which Elizabeth plunged as the Kings Norton candidate. Her political faith was still rooted in the Liberal philosophy—her object was "the greatest happiness of the greatest number," and the means to that achievement as she saw it lay in freedom of thought, of choice, of trade, of discussion, with the tacit assumption that through the clash of ideas and interests an ultimate harmony would result. Until she entered the political arena she was unaware how deep was the fissure which had opened between the old Liberal creed and the newer forms of left-wing ideology. The doctrine of the class war and an inevitable and irreconcilable antagonism of interests had bitten deeply into the thought of the Labour Party of the day. Control of the means of production, not philanthropy or even co-partnership; to build afresh, not to reform; to search for the new forms of economic and social organization demanded by a shrinking world where an intense national self-consciousness was issuing in unwonted restrictions and organized violence; to find security in an age of crisis—these were the demands of the new radicals of the left, Socialists, Fabians, Trade Unionists.

Elizabeth came forward with a programme which included freedom of trade, the improvement of housing, progressive legislation in the departments of public health, education, and child welfare, the remodelling of the Old Age Pensions Act, and enlarged schemes of road-making, railway extensions, land reclamation, and housing to absorb the rapidly growing ranks of the unemployed. Her election address was thus a mixture of new and old, embodying along with reform and individual freedom a demand for increasing security and a policy of full employment which foreshadowed the concept of the Social Welfare State.

She went before her constituents with the desire to put forward ideas that she believed to be constructive and educational. She discovered how few people, unfortunately, were desirous of being made to think; "the majority prefer tub-thumping," was her comment. Professor Gilbert Murray, Professor Pigou (the economist), Sir Willoughby Dickinson, H. A. L. Fisher (the historian), and Professor H. G. Wood were among the speakers who appeared on her platform, men who could explain the historical reasons for the Liberal policy and who could speak with knowledge of economic and social problems and programmes. Her Conservative opponents, whose candidate was Sir Herbert Austin, fought mainly on the issue of tariff reform, which appealed particularly to the Midland manufacturers. A few days before the poll it was widely circulated in the Birmingham neighbourhood that most of the works would close down in six months if the Conservatives, pledged to Protection, were not returned, and this undoubtedly influenced the 'floating vote' at the last moment.

Elizabeth had always had great sympathy with the Labour Party (which at one time she had seriously thought of joining), so that the utterances and tactics of her Labour opponents, revealing how deep was the rift in thought between them, came as a great shock. But, having entered the ring, however distasteful she found it, she resolutely stayed the course. Night by night she attended her political meetings, speaking with her customary incisiveness, calling on her ready wit to deal good-humouredly with the hecklers, always striving to appeal to the intelligence rather than to rouse the emotions of her audience. Wherever she went she found friends in every corner of the Division, and the children would swarm out to greet her, whatever colours they were wearing.

Elizabeth had only agreed to stand at all after much pressure from the local Liberals, "but my decision," she says, "was also influenced by the messages and encouragement I received from many societies, both national and international, and also from many individuals up and down the country, interested in social questions with which I am connected. I came forward, therefore, rather as a representative of certain ideas and ideals, than as a typical partisan." She still, as twenty years before, saw the dangers of a rigid party doctrine, particularly in a moment of national crisis such as her country was facing; the experience of the election campaign confirmed and strengthened that perception.

The polling day in Birmingham ended in a thick fog, which damped the hopes of her ardent and faithful band of workers, Leonard Appleton, her agent, the late Harold Watts, personnel manager of the Bournville Works, her sons, nephews, and sons-in-law, and a large number of her friends. The Liberal organization even then was weak in Birmingham; "we had really no Party to call upon, only personal votes," Elizabeth Cadbury confesses. On the day of the count it was quickly apparent that Sir Herbert Austin was the winning candidate. She took defeat in her stride: "I was soon back in work again, as the same afternoon I had my Hygiene Committee where I was met by officials in the Education office with cheers and congratulations that I was not leaving them for a seat in Parliament," she wrote in her family letter. "The work and devotion of innumerable loyal and devoted personal friends entirely counterbalanced any sense of failure. We feel the need of real educational work throughout the neighbourhood. Whether we can reinstate the Liberal Party here I do not know." Her experience served only to strengthen her faith in the principles and functions of that Party, which, she believed, strove for an all-embracing and imaginative vision of the needs of the people as a whole, and not of one section or class, while class warfare, she felt, "will destroy the whole spirit of citizenship." She was also confirmed in her belief that an ethical and religious basis was essential for political action, and was impatient of doctrinaire theories, or of what George Fox would have called mere "notions."

As Elizabeth felt that the political field was closed to her, her public service on the wider stage of world affairs was henceforth given to movements for peace and international co-operation and for a closer fellowship between the Churches. But the immediate needs of her city and neighbourhood were never forgotten; her work for education, for health, and for the hospital service of her city continued unabated and grew despite the increasing weight of years.

The work carried on in and around the Selly Oak Colleges was steadily expanding, and it became clear that a central meeting-place would be a very great asset to the life of the student community. In 1927 Elizabeth met this need by building a central hall as a memorial to her husband. It was named the George Cadbury Hall, and was designed by Hubert Lidbetter to seat 500 people; the site on the crest of Griffin's Hill was given by her stepson George. The Hall was dedicated in an opening ceremony on October 28 in that year. Elizabeth Cadbury, in handing the building over to the Central Council of the Selly Oak Colleges, stated that it would be used for the purposes for which the Colleges existed—namely, for the study of religious and social problems, and to give opportunity to men and women to equip themselves for the service of God and their fellow-men. It would also be available for recreation, for stimulating interest in art, music, literature, and the drama.

In the War of 1939–45 the hall was requisitioned by the Ministry of Works to house the Women's Exchange of the Ministry of Labour. In 1947 Elizabeth set to work to get the building released for the use of the Colleges once more. It was almost entirely due to her efforts that the hall was freed by the spring of 1948, and this involved much patient and at times outspoken correspondence with the Ministries concerned, with the local Member of Parliament, with the trustees of the Selly Oak Institute, to which the Employment Exchange was finally transferred, and with the Education Department in Birmingham. All this she carried on week by week with unwearied persistence.

The removal of the Exchange, when it at length took place in February 1948, involved the displacement of a flourishing youth club at the Selly Oak Institute, which had to be content with inadequate premises in the school at Raddlebarn Lane, adjoining the Estate. This caused much anxiety to Elizabeth.

The club leader wrote with some bitterness to the Trustees of the Institute, suggested that "cold, calculating heads" were now ruling in places where there had formerly been a warm human sympathy "and that is where we start (socially) the downward path." Elizabeth Cadbury, however, sought an interview with him to explain the situation in person. He found her deeply concerned and grieved over the displacement of his boys, trying to weigh fairly the counter-claims of the Selly Oak Colleges and the Youth Club, anxious to meet him as a friend and to consider fully his problems and desires. He was completely won over, and left with the sense that the challenge of new difficulties might serve to strengthen the service of his club members. So infectious still was the courage and humanity of Elizabeth at the age of fourscore years and ten.

12

Service to the Birmingham Hospitals— and a Chapter of Accidents

ELIZABETH CADBURY'S interests in the closely allied subjects of health and housing date back to the days of her young womanhood. She has left it on record that it was Florence Nightingale's appeal for girls of good education to take up nursing as a profession that first drew her attention to the service given by the public hospitals. Her sister Janet was one of those who responded to the appeal, and while she was serving as a probationer in the Victoria Hospital for children at Chelsea young Elsie Taylor frequently visited her there, taking flowers and presents for the children and seeing a little of the life in the wards. Her parents were much interested in the establishment of the National Temperance Hospital in 1880, and Elizabeth herself became President of this in the mid-nineteen-thirties.

She visited Florence Nightingale on several occasions, the last time only a few weeks before her death. The first occasion was in 1904, when she found her looking "very sweet, with white shawls and beautiful lace, and she was most keen and interested in everything I told her. She was anxious to hear all about our village [Bournville], and when I tried to refer to her own great work she waved it aside and would hardly speak of it."

The inspiration of that great pioneer remained with Elizabeth, and her opportunity to serve the crippled children of her city through the establishment of the Woodlands Hospital was especially welcome because of her memories of Florence Nightingale. The work of the Woodlands developed rapidly from the mid-twenties. In 1919 Mr Wilson Stuart came to Birmingham and began his long association with the hospital as the successor of Mr Dunn. Elizabeth found in him a fellow worker who shared her enthusiasm for the education of the children and who was equally desirous of training his nurses to a high standard. She welcomed his ardour, and supported and aided his plans. Her mind was always alert, receptive, able to embrace the new idea, the unrealized vision, or perhaps, said Mr Wilson Stuart, the new could be achieved because her thought had already run ahead to grasp the possibility emerging before others were yet aware of it.

In the year 1925 the Birmingham Cripples Union and the Royal Orthopædic and Spinal Hospital for adults agreed to amalgamate and become known henceforth as the Royal Cripples Hospital. The work of the Orthopædic Hospital had been carried on hitherto in Newhall Street in Birmingham, but plans were set on foot in the latter twenties to remove the in-patients to the Woodlands on the outskirts of the city. Extensions to the Woodlands were put in hand on land given by Elizabeth, and in 1929 the change took place. The number of beds at the Woodlands was brought up to one hundred, a new operating theatre and Physiotherapy Department were built, and a nurses' home with accommodation for fifty nurses.

The Duchess of York (now the Queen Mother) opened these additional premises in November 1929. To the recently appointed matron, Miss F. R. Smith, who came just before the amalgamation, fell the difficult and delicate task of uniting the two sections of the new institution, getting the staffs to work together in harmony as a team, and meeting the very varying needs of the adult and child patients. The success of the enlarged and different Woodlands was to a great extent due to her skilled and devoted service over twenty years. In that work she had behind her the loyal support, the patient understanding, of Elizabeth Cadbury.[1]

It was not, however, her work as chairman in guiding these developments, her generosity as a donor, or her ability in organizing appeals, fêtes, 'miles of pennies,' and similar activities to raise

[1] There has been steady and quiet development at the Woodlands since 1929, including the additions of a staff recreation hall, a nurses' lecture hall (the gift of Elizabeth Cadbury), a surgeon's house, and a number of private wards. In 1938 a hostel for the domestic staff was opened, called the Dame Elizabeth Cadbury Home, and the men's and women's wards were enlarged, this work being completed in 1940. Elizabeth Cadbury gave a generous donation, and the women's ward is named after her.

funds for the hospital, that are the first memories recalled by the matron and staff of the Woodlands. It is again Elizabeth, the person, in her contact with patients and nurses and committee members, who is remembered with affection, with admiration, with a warm gladness. She would come into the hospital at all hours, watchful and sensitive to the needs of the children whom she loved, always with some special word of comfort and of healing to any child or adult who was particularly ill. She had so won the confidence of matron and nurses that they could turn to her freely in any moment of difficulty or tension. She was always available, somehow, with all her multifarious activities, to give a hearing and wise counsel to a matron harassed by the heedless behaviour of a young probationer, kicking against the discipline of hospital life. If need be, Elizabeth would go over to the Woodlands herself to have a talk with the recalcitrant— explaining carefully at the beginning of the interview that as a mother and grandmother of a large family she understood some at least of the difficulties of youth. Always, it is the testimony of the matron, those interviews had good results, and there was a changed attitude towards her work and responsibilities on the part of the nurse thereafter.

Elizabeth had enjoyed such abounding good health throughout her life that when the test of sickness and of failing powers came to her it was all the harder for her to accept that discipline with patience. But it gave her deeper insight into the needs of the sick, a closer understanding and sympathy with which to set about her work for them.

In the middle of January 1926 sinus trouble, with which she had been threatened for some months, became suddenly acute. Three operations had to be performed within the course of the next few weeks. In great pain, and with the first operation looming ahead, she persisted in fulfilling her engagement to broadcast the Sunday evening address on January 24.

"I do not intend to give any sort of indication of the kind of things that I had to endure," she wrote on March 4, 1926.

Even now I have a visit from one doctor in the morning and another in the evening, for treatment, and I feel as though it has been

K

going on for years, so that I look forward greatly to the day when I shall be free again. All I can say is, that if any of my friends or family wish to indulge in an operation, I advise them not to choose this particular species. The strain was, of course, in this particular case increased by the fact of having three different tries, and twice having to leave home, and both those last times wondering, as I went down the drive, whether I should return. I mention these points by way of contrast, as I also want to record the spiritual and mental help I received from so many well-wishers.

Four years later came a yet greater test to her courage and patience. In the autumn of 1930 Elizabeth stumbled and fell heavily on the stairs at the Manor, but insisted upon carrying out a round of engagements in the next few days, including attendance at the annual meetings of the National Council of Women at Portsmouth. On November 17 she writes:

I, who very much object to interviews with doctors, have been finding out how many different kinds there are in Birmingham. Unfortunately the fall or something seems to have affected my sight and I find great difficulty in reading, and therefore have been oscillating between a radiographer, an oculist, an orthopædist, a nerve specialist and an aurist, finishing up with the radiographer again, who remarked that he was 'Alpha and Omega'! The joint opinion is that an antrum has been injured in some way, and that it must be dealt with. I have received preliminary attention twice but am having the more drastic treatment on Saturday next.

This had no effect, and early in December Elizabeth consulted Sir William Lister, who arranged for her to enter a nursing home in Wimpole Street immediately for treatment under his direction. Henry Cadbury arranged for Eiluned Lewis[1] to come in daily to read aloud to his mother. "She has stayed at a hotel close by," wrote Elizabeth Cadbury, "and comes every day attending to letters, arranging my visitors, and reading aloud. The latter is a special boon in the evenings, as how I could have spent the long hours without being able to read I can't imagine."

The treatment was continued at home, including a period of

[1] Eiluned Lewis, the author, had formerly acted as reader to Henry Cadbury, when his own eyes were too bad to permit of his reading to himself.

complete rest in one room at the Manor, under the care of a nurse. Radiant-heat baths were also part of the course prescribed and continued until early in February, when the nerve specialist who came to see how she was standing them "knocked them off for some little time; he thinks few people could have stood them so long."

But all was in vain, and Elizabeth was faced with rapidly fading sight, so that the last twenty years of her life were passed in a condition of near-blindness. She was quite unable to read, and could distinguish colours only by closely peering at a bank of flowers or a length of fabric. People were but hazy outlines to her. Yet few who encountered her in those last decades of her life realized how limited was her range of vision, for she refused to allow herself to be handicapped by this grave disability or to curtail her activities and the pace of her daily round.

A further serious physical burden was laid upon her when she was over eighty years of age. Elizabeth was travelling to Mentone in January 1939, taking with her for a holiday her youngest daughter Ursula, her companion Elsa Fox, her nephew Brian Taylor, a young doctor, and a medical friend of his, Dr D'Abreu. As the train ran into the Gare de Lyons in Paris the conductor called out that there would be only a ten-minute stop. Elizabeth, impatient for a little fresh air and exercise, was waiting with a little knot of people by the door, and, seeing the man in front of her step out on to the platform, thought that the train had already come to a halt while it was, in fact, still moving gently. She, therefore, herself stepped off, "and the next I knew I was lying in a shattered heap on the platform with my nose a few inches from the wheels," she tells us.

Brian Taylor and Dr D'Abreu lifted her back into the Wagons-lit, and quickly diagnosed that her hip was broken. A hurried consultation took place as to what was to be done, but Elizabeth Cadbury, with a vivid recollection of the Paris hospitals she had known in her youth, insisted on continuing her journey to Mentone. Throughout the night, though in great pain, she talked cheerfully to the two young men who sat up with her in turn. A telegram from Marseilles brought an ambulance to the train to meet her, and she was quickly installed in her bedroom at the Riviera Palace Hotel. A special anæsthetic was flown from London, the leg was set, and for the next few weeks Elizabeth Cadbury lay in bed, insisting that her young companions should carry out their programme of sight-seeing and enjoyment and should not curtail their holiday. Then came the difficult journey back to England, when she was lifted on a stretcher to and fro through the wide windows of the Continental trains, and finally was brought to the Royal Northern Hospital in London. But she was chafing to get home; the succession of nurses she found confusing, kind though they all were, and after a few days she rang up her nephew Brian from her bed, to demand that he arrange for her to be taken back to the Manor. Wisely he acceded to her wishes without argument, a conference with the hospital authorities smoothed out the difficulties, and on February 3 she returned home in an ambulance, to the joy of being in her own room at the Manor, with two nurses from the Woodlands to attend her, and Mr Wilson Stuart and Dr Jeyes to take charge of the case.

The London surgeon had wanted to put a Peterson's pin through the thigh, and had inserted a pin below the knee, with a weight on the end of the leg to keep it straight. Elizabeth did not like the idea of the pin in the thigh, which would mean a stiffened leg for the rest of her life, and Mr Wilson Stuart agreed to her request that this should not be done. Shortly after her return home he removed the pin below the knee, an operation he performed without an anæsthetic because of her sinus trouble. "How she stood it I do not know," he said, "but she did, without a cry." The thigh-bone never again joined up, but in time Elizabeth Cadbury could walk with only a slight limp. At ninety, striding round her garden, she would pause to ask the visitor of the moment, who might be half a century her junior, if she were going too quickly for that companion's comfort! Her complete confidence in her doctors, the skilful and devoted nursing she received, the care of her companion and daughters, and, above all, the delight of being at home quickly restored her to health. Within a few weeks she was attending the Bourn-ville Meeting for Worship and the Bournville Trust in a wheelchair; a little later and she was hobbling about in a calliper, with the aid of crutches or two sticks. She even persisted in bathing that summer, leaving the calliper on the beach and hopping into the water supported by her daughter Dorothea and her faithful chauffeur, Tutton. She was staying in the holiday house which Dorothea and Geoffrey Hoyland had taken at Trebetherick in Cornwall; her car would be driven over the sands as near to the sea as was safe, and then the bathe would take place. Once the advancing tide nearly overwhelmed the car, whose wheels had sunk in the sand, and it was only rescued at the last moment, with the aid of another bathing party and some planks. But Elizabeth Cadbury sat by, chuckling, and enjoying the adventure

Despite her lameness and her loss of sight Elizabeth Cadbury nevertheless accepted the invitation given to her in 1941 to become President of the United Hospitals in Birmingham, which included the Queen Elizabeth Hospital and Medical School in Edgbaston, and the General Hospital in the city. She held this position till July 1948, when the National Health Service came into operation. To her this position was no sinecure. She presided at the Annual Meetings of the Board of Governors, memorizing the long agenda beforehand as she could not see to read it, and going over the business in advance with the Secretary of the United Hospitals Committee, Mr Herford. "Only very occasionally would she have to refer to me at the meetings for the name of a proposer or seconder, or for some other small point on the agenda that had slipped her memory," he said, in speaking of her work for the hospitals. She was always present most regularly at social functions, distributing medals and certificates at the annual prize-givings to the nurses, attending the hospital dances, slipping into the wards unannounced at all sorts of odd moments, to talk with the patients and staff, discover any wants or needs, and to cheer and strengthen by the mere fact of her bracing presence. Not even the brutal weather of the winter of 1947 could prevent her appearance at the nurses' dance at the Queen Elizabeth! When she had fallen in London and broken her wrist she arrived next day at the prize-giving ceremony at the General Hospital, though obviously in pain; she carried through the proceedings with her usual cheerfulness, and when she discovered that no arrangement had been made to close the gathering, said briskly, "We can't do better than end it with the doxology," to the astonishment of some of the doctors, and started off the singing herself. On two occasions she broadcast an appeal. Once it was in the Week's Good Cause on Sunday evening—a plea for support for the United Hospitals of Birmingham, to which she herself brought in her own contribution on the following day; and once, a few months before the nationalization of the Health Services, on the opening of the Staff and Patients Amenities Funds. "It is extremely interesting to watch the gradual development of this vast scheme," she wrote of the United Hospitals, "and to learn of the fresh ideas being considered and carried out for those who suffer in many ways."

Her own experiences of sickness and of pain only increased her concern for the welfare of the hospital service, her understanding of those who came to seek its aid, her desire that it might be efficient and *human*. When the nationalization of the hospitals was completed and there was no longer need for the voluntary effort that had built them up and maintained them for so many years, her one fear was that the service might become a vast, efficient machine, entirely impersonal. For she knew that the human personality would shrink within "the cold embrace of officialdom." Her own close friendship with her doctors and surgeons had been such a strengthening power in the long days of pain that she realized its inestimable value in helping a patient over the rough places of convalescence. Could a State medical service maintain those personal relationships, give the doctor time to build up in his patients the quiet confidence in his skill and effort that were half the battle on the road to recovery? It was with these questions in mind that she faced the new era, accepting still with interest, if with some regrets, the changing world about her that heralded the approach of her ninetieth birthday.

13

Religious Experience and Faith

ALL the busy round of daily duties and self-imposed tasks, the untiring service which Elizabeth Cadbury gave to her fellows, sprang from her deep-rooted faith, her immediate knowledge, of the living power of God moving in the spirit of man.

She had been brought up, as we have seen, a member of the Society of Friends at a period when it was deeply influenced by the Evangelical Movement. But she moved beyond the narrower confines of that thought without losing the quickening impulse which was the strength of the Evangelical experience. She welcomed the fresh discoveries, the application of the methods of historical criticism which brought a changed and deeper understanding of the Bible in the latter decades of the nineteenth century. She herself was a diligent reader of the books of Scripture, and in her visits to those in trouble or suffering it was in the words of Scripture, tested throughout the ages in the experience of men, that she found the counsel or the consolation to pass on to the perplexed and stricken. But her alert, questioning mind was open to receive the truth from whatever source it came. "Buddha and Confucius and certainly the Moslem religion have something to tell us," she wrote in a letter to a friend in 1938. From the Greek philosophers, especially Plato, from the plays of Shakespeare, the essays of Ruskin, the poetry of Wordsworth and Browning, she drew fresh inspiration in her search to discover for herself the good life. For those who "divide life into compartments, and decide for themselves that only one compartment is pleasing to God," she had little time. "God is best served when every side of our complete being (and thinking) is developed; when the intellect as well as the emotions are cultivated, so that our faith may rest on a broad and reasonable basis, not too hemmed in by creed and dogma," she wrote in 1899.

But as the Society threw off the shackles of its Puritan and narrow Evangelical tradition she saw it exposed to new dangers. The vision captured by the younger leaders of thought at the turn of the century gradually faded. The thought-provoking, serious, and living ministry, which it had been hoped that Woodbrooke would foster, failed to make its appearance. There was a retreat on the part of the Society's younger members from business to the professions, particularly to teaching in the pre-1914 years. In the period between the wars and after 1945 more and more sought their life's work in some form of social service. The great contribution which the Quakers of the nineteenth century had made to the industrial and financial life of the country was largely missing after 1900. The emphasis of the Society's thought and utterances was on the need for world peace, and the attempt to build up a surer foundation for international and racial relationships.

After the war of 1914, out of the large-scale relief work undertaken on the Continent of Europe by American and English Friends, came the birth of 'Quaker embassies' or centres in many of the Continental capitals and chief cities, where the task of forging links of friendship and understanding between the nations could be carried on. At home the years of the great depression and wide-spread unemployment led to fresh ventures of relief, of education, and attempts at reconstruction in the coalfields of South Wales. The question of the basis on which industry should be reorganized, of the discovery of true human relations within industry, became important and interesting but almost entirely academic questions to the bulk of the Society's members, who were withdrawn from the actual field of struggle and experiment. For lack of a first-hand knowledge of industrial and economic problems discussions of these matters were often somewhat thin and 'in the air,' or touched with doctrinaire passion. Friends were genuinely concerned with the evils of world conditions, with the growth of international jealousy and strife, with the inequalities and injustices of the social system at home, and the dark, terrible cloud of unemployment. But there was lacking knowledge, a depth of spiritual experience, and the essential, selfless dedication which alone could have enabled them to clear a path through the tangle of confused thought that enveloped the nations, and to act with decision, imagination, and creative power.

Elizabeth saw these trends clearly, and with growing concern. Religion to her was first and foremost eminently practical. "After wrangling for centuries over creeds and forms of worship, Christendom is struggling to the perception of the truth that the amount of care we have for our neighbour is the gauge of our Christianity, and not the orthodoxy of our belief," she wrote in the early years of the twentieth century. "And what does our neighbour want? He wants justice more than charity."

The centre and core of the Quaker experience and expression of faith lies in the Meeting for Worship. To Elizabeth, the Friends' method of waiting together in silence before God offered the widest field for spiritual growth and opportunity for adventure. If it were rightly held, she said, the Meeting demanded of its members a great unselfishness. So many came desiring something for themselves, or with their minds burdened with problems which would face them in the coming week, and were not really prepared to wait for the guidance of the Holy Spirit and communion with the living God. She pleaded for a liberty which would allow expression in a hymn of praise and thanksgiving, for, without desiring any set programme of service, she felt that Friends lost much by omitting all music from their gatherings. In the Meeting at Bournville one hymn at least was sung during the hour of worship, and any member was free to ask for a hymn which he felt would give voice to the experience of the meeting at that moment.

The problem of arousing and stimulating an effective ministry in the Quaker meeting was one which much exercised her thought. "The condition of the individual meeting varies more than is probably the case with other branches of the Christian Church; Friends are encouraged to think for themselves as members of a spiritual democracy and are perhaps inclined to foster individualistic tendencies," she once wrote. Again, Quakers, she noted, were apt to pride themselves on their unconventionality, and to consider that the solution of any problem, if it commended itself to another section of the Church, must necessarily be wrong for the Society of Friends. All these things made the question of a living vocal ministry a particularly difficult one for the Society, a problem which is still unsolved.

But though her roots were deep in the Quaker tradition and experience, and her mind was much exercised with its problems, Elizabeth's outlook was œcumenical rather than sectarian. As we have seen in a previous chapter, she had been in the forefront of the endeavour to bring Nonconformists of the country into a closer fellowship. In the early twenties, as the possibility of a yet larger fraternity developed which would embrace both the Anglican and Greek Orthodox Churches, Elizabeth again was one of the first members of the Society of Friends to see the significance and hope of these trends.

In the summer of 1924 she was present at a Conference of the Churches in Mürren, called to consider the question of "Our Common Evangel." Sir Henry Lunn had invited representatives from all sections of the Christian Church in Europe to attend the gathering, and nearly one hundred accepted. Among the speakers were the Provost of Trinity College, Dublin, the Bishops of Winchester, Chichester, Peterborough, Chelmsford and Plymouth, the Archbishop of Uppsala, Primate of Sweden, Bishop Nikolai of the Orthodox Church of Serbia, Bishop Ravasz of Hungary, Dr Adolf Deissman and Dr Julius Richter of the Lutheran Church in Germany, Dr Scott Lidgett, Dr T. R. Glover, Dr Carnegie Simpson, and Sir Donald Maclean from various branches of the Church in Great Britain. Elizabeth Cadbury had been attacked by severe pain in the head and behind her eyes a week or so before the conference, the trouble which a year later was to result in a series of operations. But she refused to let this interfere with her plans, and arrived at the gathering accompanied by her young niece Joy Clarke, and by Joyce Ilbert, but with her eyes still aching somewhat. However, within two days she went off on a long walk with a party of twenty, and was out for nearly nine hours, as they got badly lost in a dense wood. "We spent an immense time following up various clues, and climbing up and down hills and falling into bogs and crevasses, and finally found ourselves near the railway after the last train had passed," she wrote home on September 4.

"Two of our party were rather exhausted, so a doctor and I got into the deserted station, telephoned Lauterbrunnen and asked them to send a train along, which they did in about ten minutes, very smart, and we were back at 8.0, very late for dinner, and jokes have been kept up since about the danger of Episcopal guidance." She adds, with complacency, "I was amazed that I managed the expedition without being tired; my only difficulty being when the various bishops *would* ask me to expound Quaker doctrine when we were climbing up-hill."

Soon after she had arrived at Mürren the President of the conference asked Elizabeth Cadbury if she would take part in the proceedings, and after some hesitation she agreed to give an address on George Fox. She had with her a recent edition of his Journal, and with her remembrance of that and of his life-long preaching "managed to put together a paper." Rather to her astonishment, there was what she describes as a huge attendance at her lecture: "I felt fearfully nervous," she confesses; "however, everyone was most kind and appreciative, and it has given me acquaintance with nearly every one in the place. Another rather amusing result is that nearly every speaker since has alluded to the Quaker position!" It was not an easy audience to address; "some of the nonconformists bristle all over when the Anglo-Catholics get on the warpath with the claims of the Catholic Church, or refer to Confession or their view of the Sacraments," she commented on some of the earlier discussions. Among the contingent from the Continent was Sabatier, the great student of St Francis, and from America Dr Moffat, the translator of the Bible into modern speech. Studdert Kennedy had arrived a little late; these were among the assembly of scholars and clergy who faced Elizabeth Cadbury on that late summer's afternoon, critical if friendly—always looking with some puzzlement at the representatives of the odd little Society of Friends, called Quakers, who stood outside the more familiar ranks of Nonconformity.

To that company Elizabeth Cadbury spoke of George Fox's discovery of the inner, spiritual nature of man which bore a seed or spark of the divine, and of the way opened thereby for the human being to come into direct relationship with God. There was no need of the mediation of priest or clergymen. On the basis of that experience of the life of God moving in the human spirit Fox rested his religious structure, and challenged the whole prevailing thought of his age. He could not accept the authority of an infallible Church or Book, of tradition or dogmatism. Revelation was continuous, said Elizabeth Cadbury, and was not confined to a limited dispensation, nor was it limited to the Bible. The Bible itself was not to be regarded as the holy book whose every phrase and sentence must be taken as the literal word of God, and as containing all the spiritual truth that man will ever need to know or can know. Fox turned from all such conceptions, asserting that the day-dawn is continually coming, and "the day-star is for ever rising in men's hearts."[1] To Calvin's doctrine of original sin as the native "seed" in man he opposed the simple statement that "The Lord opened to me by His invisible power that every man was enlightened by the Divine Light of Christ."

Such was the theme of Elizabeth Cadbury's address, her words of necessity challenging the closely held beliefs, the cherished convictions of most of her audience. She ventured further in an attempt to explain the Quaker attitude towards the innermost sanctities of the established churches symbolized in the Eucharist.

"Fox's position with regard to the Sacrament of the Lord's Supper is too big a question to enter into fully," she said,

> but we may consider one phase of his thought regarding its significance. He stated as his belief that as Christians got deeper into the spiritual life they would find the outward Sacrament unnecessary. His rejection involved a definite view of the nature of the growth of development of Christian experience. "For," he said, "after ye have eaten in the remembrance of His death, then ye must come into His death and die with Him if ye will live with Him as the Apostles did—and that is a nearer and a further state, to be in fellowship with Him in His death than to take Bread and Wine in remembrance of His death."

The reception accorded to her at the close of her address suggests that her very diverse audience appreciated the courage and sincerity with which she spoke.

A year later, in 1925, she was elected President of the Federal

[1] Rufus Jones.

Council of the Free Churches. She was the first, and so far has been the only, woman to hold this office. During her year as President she travelled to the north, south, east, and west of the country, speaking to the local branches of the Free Church Council in different districts. She was anxious to recall to her audience the fact that all through the ages the Church and the followers of Christ generally had cared for the social betterment of the world, and not only for the welfare of their souls. It was very encouraging to her to see the part played by the women in the movement, and that in some places it was the women who were keeping the interest alive and exploring new avenues of inter-Church fellowship. "The times call for strenuous and intelligent workers, but still more for devoted men and women of Faith and Prayer, who by their lives will proclaim the gospel of peace to the harassed, distrustful and burdened peoples of the world." Letters of appreciation poured in from the towns and cities that she visited, thanking her for her messages and the encouragement and inspiration they had left among the community.

In July, during the year of her presidency, she arranged for two summer schools for ministers to be held at Woodbrooke, the members coming by her invitation as her guests. H. G. Wood, the Director of Studies at Woodbrooke,[1] and his wife acted as wardens for her. She also held a "quiet day" at the Manor House for ministers and their wives belonging to the West Midland Federation and the Birmingham and District Free Church Council. Some eighty-five ministers attended the latter, and seventy were present at the Summer Schools, representing all shades of thought and various grades of experience. "When we talk together what a fund of information we gather, what sidelights on big movements, what glimpses of great men," wrote one of the Summer School students. "As for the lectures, could there have been a better, a more practical or fruitful series? The seventy ministers here will treasure the happiest memories of this week, for this has been a term of true schooling, a widening of horizons, and a 'season of refreshment from the presence of the Lord.' "

[1] Later he held the Chair of Theology at Birmingham University.

Meanwhile the wider œcumenical movement was gathering momentum, and one of those most interested and giving stimulus o the venture was Dr William Temple, later to become the Archbishop of Canterbury. The first explorations had been made in the field of missionary enterprise earlier in the century, beginning with the International Missionary Conference held at Edinburgh in 1910. Many of the Christian leaders saw the danger of the churches seeking to come to a closer understanding on matters of faith and methods of worship while remaining isolated from the problems of social and international life. Among these men was Nathan Söderblom, Archbishop of Uppsala, who sought for a means whereby the mind and the conscience of the Christian world might find expression on the social, industrial, and national questions that were rending the peoples asunder into separate and hostile camps. Could not the Churches try to discover the immediate bearing of the Christian faith on the social and international order, and give much-needed guidance and direction to the counsels of the politicians and industrialists? For six years preparations were made for a World Conference on "Christian Life and Work," and this met in Stockholm in the year 1925, when more than five hundred representatives of the greater number of Christian communions met together. Elizabeth was invited to attend as President of the Free Church Council, and went to take her seat beside the patriarchs and archbishops of the National and Orthodox Churches. "The Archbishop of Uppsala is most energetic and ubiquitous, and seems kindly to consider me under his charge," Elizabeth Cadbury wrote to her family from Stockholm, on August 23. "The subject on the first day was—'The Church and Economic and Industrial Problems.' The Archbishop rather suddenly asked me to take part in the discussions. The question had arisen as to whether Christianity and modern industry were compatible, so I sketched what methods might be adopted in an ideal state. . . ." Elizabeth had been asked beforehand to give a paper on Housing to the assembly, and this came a few days later. Though she found the length and number of the speeches rather wearisome, she was constantly aware of the significance of the gathering; "It is a wonderful thing that it has happened at all; 1600 years since the Greek Church met with the Roman. On Sunday we all journeyed in a special train, 300 of all nations, tribes and tongues, to Uppsala. A fine picturesque service in the Cathedral, 5000 present—the Nicene Creed, compiled at the previous great œcumenical Council in 325 A.D., recited by the Orthodox, Beatitudes in Greek, and fine congregational singing in four languages," she notes in her journal.

The first World Conference on Faith and Order took place at Lausanne two years later, and in this branch of the movement also Elizabeth took a keen interest. A second meeting was held at Edinburgh in 1937 under the chairmanship of the English archbishop, William Temple. The Society of Friends was represented on the Commission set up in Great Britain to carry on the task of discussion and clarification between the meetings of the World Conferences and appointed its own committee to keep the subject under review.

Elizabeth was convinced that Friends had much to learn from other members of the Christian confession. She perceived with growing uneasiness how vague and unanchored was the thought of the modern Society of Friends. It was to her lasting regret that London Yearly Meeting felt unable to join the World Council of Churches when plans for its establishment were set on foot in 1938 to supersede and combine the work of the Conferences and Continuation Committees on Faith and Order and Life and Work. Even the simple credal basis of the World Council as "a fellowship of Churches which accept our Lord Jesus Christ as God and Saviour," proved a stumbling-block to the twentieth-century Quaker. He refused to submit his faith to a simple dogmatic statement, and with his three-hundred-year-old suspicion of anything that smacked of a creed he preferred to stand aloof from the movement. Of the dangers inherent in this sincerely held position Elizabeth was keenly aware. "Friends are so inclined to pride themselves on the nebulousness of their faith," she wrote in a letter to Carl Heath in the autumn of 1940.

There is a danger of our becoming something like the balloons that are at present swaying backwards and forwards round every big city, which, if they were not attached to a foundation on the

earth, would roam the skies, a danger to themselves and others.
. . . Individuals waver in their adherence to various religious
dogmas, but surely there must be some fundamental points on which
to build a Christian Society.

To some minds the only thing that appears to matter is our
testimony with regard to peace and war. Applicants for membership
in some Meetings are considered to have passed the test if they
are clear on that particular doctrine. . . .

But the Society of Friends was neither a peace organization
nor a league of social service. It was a religious community, a
branch of the Christian Church, which must stand or fall by the
depth and reality of the spiritual life of its members. Were
Friends, she asked, so given over to "good works" or absorbed
by political and international problems that they forgot this
fact, and were unable therefore to meet and pray with others?
Ministry in the Meetings for Worship, she felt, had become
theoretic, idealistic, or largely concerned with social questions;
there were signs that the scientific humanism of the age was
penetrating the thought of Quakerism, and many were adopting
the Unitarian position. The living, prophetic Word, the preaching of the gospel of Christ, were lamentably absent, in her
opinion.

Against that drift, that growing misty vagueness of belief,
she set her own faith built upon the experience of God realized
throughout the lengthening years of her life. To the patient,
steady seeker she said:

The God whom the thinkers and dreamers of centuries were
pursuing, stands at last revealed in the person of a Man, one of
ourselves, with human form, human desires and affections and
temptations, but His Son, to use our human language; and to our
perplexed and clouded and stupid brains He says: "I am the Way,
the Truth and the Life." Just what we want; a Way in which to
walk, a goal to which to steer; Truth, the all-important alchemy
of life, and Life—life more abundant, fuller, deeper, richer. During
two years He devoted Himself to explaining the meaning of these
words to the men He had chosen to be with Him. . . . By His
death and resurrection, He found His divinity and kingship. Not
only by words but by His life, He showed forth the love, the pity,
the strength, the purity and the righteousness of God.

Even when she was nearing her seventieth year it was still the young Christ in the joy and vigour of His manhood who most clearly represented to Elizabeth the incarnate God. In the broadcast address which she gave on January 24, 1926, on the eve of her first serious operation, she tells us that she pictured Him as the very incarnation of the spirit of youth—humorous, witty, a clever craftsman, and an interesting, stimulating companion, filled at moments with an exhilarating *joie de vivre*, able to share to the full in the absorbing details of daily life and friendship. It was her comprehension of the abiding presence of God, opened to men in that life, discoverable to them through the indwelling spirit of His truth, that Elizabeth shared with her listeners in that hour of her own pain and darkness. It was that presence which she *knew*, which she had tested and tried in her thought, in her battles with self-will and the love of power, in her encounter with all types and conditions of men, friendly and hostile, arrogant and stupid, bright or dull-witted, in her hours of loneliness and disappointment, and the unassuaged sorrow of final parting from those she loved most. As she had learnt to trust and to follow the promptings of that inner Spirit, so there had opened before her ever-new roads of service and of effort, and life was for ever a continuing adventure.

14

Towards the Unity of Nations

ELIZABETH CADBURY was an active member of the National Council of Women in this country almost from its inception, and the Convener or Chairman of the Peace and Arbitration Committee of the International Council from 1914. The latter body was formed in America in the year 1880, with the hope that it might become "a republic composed of National Councils" serving as a permanent, international parliament of women where questions affecting the well-being of the individual, the family, and the commonwealth of nations might be considered from the woman's point of view.

Lady Aberdeen was President of the International Council from 1893 to 1938, and became a warm friend of Elizabeth Cadbury's in the work in which both strove so actively. The International Council held quinquennial conferences in different parts of the world, and to many of these Elizabeth travelled with eagerness in the years between the two World Wars, often accompanied by one or two of her daughters. Rome in 1914, Oslo in 1920, an Executive Committee in Copenhagen in 1924 (in which she was especially interested in a resolution urging educational authorities to interest and instruct children and young people in efforts to maintain world peace), Washington in 1925, Vienna in 1930, Dubrovnik in 1936, Brussels in 1946—Elizabeth Cadbury was present at them all. The conferences provided an opportunity to meet women of outstanding ability in various fields of activity from the four corners of the earth, to see new sparks of thought struck out in the clash of argument and discussion. She was able to encounter old friends and make many new ones, both in the official receptions and on the social occasions which were interspersed between the conference sessions and in the informal groups which gathered for tea at a private house or stole away for a motor-ride into the mountains, or for a boat-trip down fjord or lake. Elizabeth revelled in it all, keenly interested in the different customs and ways of doing things, in the strange foods, in the gay national costumes and the vigour of national folk-dances, and in attending the theatre in a strange land. Most enduring of all were the impressions made by the varied scenery she passed on her way to the conference halls in the different countries—the grey precipitous rocks of Norway, rising out of dark waters and suddenly giving place to hills covered with birch, poplar, and beech, changing from their summer green to the vivid scarlet and gold of their autumn clothing; the view from the boat steaming down the St Lawrence river in brilliant April sunshine, where the villages nestled in patches of unmelted snow on the hillsides, and a soft blue haze softened the outlines of hill and valley; the barbaric wildness of the Serbian mountains, where in each little hamlet girls stood at the roadside spinning with a distaff while watching their cattle—these were scenes that remained with her, lighting the long memory of age. Her youngest daughter, Ursula (Mrs Denis Lambert), frequently accompanied her to these quinquennial conferences, together with Miss Stuart, her governess, in the earlier days, or a young companion of her own age.

"I think my main feeling about my mother at these international gatherings was the wonderful way she had of settling difficulties and disagreements," says Ursula Lambert.

I can see her now pacing up and down at Dubrovnik with, I think, the Rumanian and Yugoslavian delegates who were at loggerheads and everything was held up because they simply could not agree. Every one else had given up all hope of a solution. There she walked with an arm through an arm of each, reasoning quietly and tactfully, and lo and behold, after a little time, the difficulty was solved and all three returned smiling.

My mother really loved all these women from many different lands, and was really interested in them. Also, her passionate desire for peace and international understanding fired them with enthusiasm too. She spoke fluent German and French, which was a tremendous advantage.

In the off-times from the conferences, she had such energy and such zest for fun or for whatever entertainment was going on, and entered into everything with her whole heart—climbing mountains in Norway, motoring over unmade roads hanging over precipices in Yugoslavia without turning a hair, while I was nearly sick with fright, thrilling with delight at the opera at Prague, or listening to a gipsy band at a fair in Budapest. Her gaiety and happiness infected others, and that helped when the serious business of the conference was on hand. She also had a quite extraordinary way of saying always exactly the right thing, even at a moment's notice, and her sense of humour very often came into what she said, convulsing others with laughter.

However haphazard the arrangements made for the delegates, and they were sometimes a little sketchy, Elizabeth would silence the grumblers by turning it all into a joke, or would sweep off her party for a ramble in the mountains while bedrooms, as yet unprepared, were got ready. Travelling to Canada in the spring of 1925, she discovered that an Atlantic crossing, even in the twentieth century, could be an adventure of some hazard. For the ship ran into a great gale, "and seemed to be first standing on end, then cracking down into the trough of the waves, lurching and rolling so wildly that many of the passengers were prepared for the worst." Elizabeth was one of the few on board who escaped seasickness, as she proudly noted. With the ship still rolling heavily she joined in a fancy-dress dance, going as Queen Elizabeth in an embroidered Chinese kimono and joining in the procession round the covered-in decks in "a more or less spasmodic fox-trot" on account of the ship's movement. Then, two days after the storm had died away, they ran into a dense fog, and for twenty-four hours the captain did not leave the bridge. Finally, as they passed out of the grey blanket of mist they were hit by a blizzard, and decks and rigging were soon covered with ice and snow, while even below deck the cold was intense. After this experience, with only one night's rest in a private home, Elizabeth and her party were plunged into a round of official receptions, public lunches, and speechmaking in Ottawa and Toronto, and then went on by way of the Niagara Falls to Washington D.C. for the International Women's Conference. The visit included a private interview for

Dame Elizabeth with President Coolidge, whom she found pleasant to talk with and easy in conversation.

On one occasion, a few days before starting on a Mediterranean cruise in the spring of 1933, Elizabeth received a message from the Foreign Office asking if she would be willing to give a lecture in Athens on behalf of the Anglo-Hellenic Society when her party reached that city. John Masefield and Dean Inge had recently addressed the Society. The subject on which she was asked to speak was "Municipal Government in Birmingham," and, feeling ready to tackle this out of hand, she agreed. She took with her a number of photographs, showing new housing estates, parks, playgrounds, and schools, and gave her lecture in the Hall of Parnassus. It was attended by many Athenians engaged in public affairs, including the deputy mayor, and Elizabeth had the opportunity of meeting several of these people beforehand at the house of the British Consul, Sir Patrick Ramsay, and found the whole experience a most interesting and stimulating one.

In 1936, when she was seventy-eight years of age, with rapidly failing eyesight, Elizabeth was asked by Lady Aberdeen to take her place in attending a conference called by the National Council of Women in India, to which delegates from various countries were invited. Intrepid as ever, and delighted with this opportunity to visit the Far East for the first time, she set off in January of that year, accompanied by her daughter Mollie, and her friend Eiluned Lewis, as her companions on this journey.

They embarked on the *Rawalpindi* at Marseilles, in a flaming sunset, and Elizabeth, still young at heart, at once entered into the spirit of adventure which a long voyage entailed for her. But on the boat she caught a bad cold and was unwell when she landed at Bombay, to be welcomed and garlanded by her Indian hostesses. Standing on the quay in the hot sun, enveloped by the strange and heavy perfumes of her flower garlands, her iron frame for once gave way, and she nearly fainted. The first receptions in Bombay she could not attend, but had to stay in bed, to her great disappointment; yet after two days' rest she insisted on continuing her journey to central India, where she had planned to visit the Quaker Mission Centres at Itarsi, Hoshangabad, and

Sohagpur. She arrived in Itarsi at 6.30 A.M. on a Sunday morning, after a night journey, and was present at the Meeting for Worship at 9.0 A.M.! Thus began the strenuous weeks of her Indian pilgrimage.

Next day, at the end of a long round of visits to schools, hostels, and Girl Guide camps in the other Quaker centres of the Central Provinces, Elizabeth found that the germ she had contracted on the boat was now attacking her ear, and she was in a good deal of pain. A visit to Benares was therefore abandoned, and she spent an extra day resting at Itarsi, but neither pain nor fatigue prevented her attending the Memorial Service for King George V held in the village. (The death of the King had occurred while she was on the voyage to India.)

On the arrival of her party in Calcutta from the Central Provinces an ear specialist was consulted; he diagnosed trouble which for most people would have meant a serious illness. But Elizabeth Cadbury felt that by that time she had overcome the difficulty. In the words of her travelling companion, Eiluned Lewis, "from then on until the end of our tour, whether speaking to school children or lunching with Governors, addressing meetings or visiting institutions, being shown the glories of India or discussing its endless problems, her immense health and energy were equal to every occasion."

In Calcutta Elizabeth reached the goal of her journey, for here the Council of Women assembled in the white-pillared Town Hall. Among the chief delegates to the Conference were the Begum Shah Nawaz, who had represented India at the League of Nations, the Maharani of Baroda, one of the greatest and most enlightened of the Indian States, and Mrs Sarojini Naidu, poet and ardent nationalist. The European delegates included the Roumanian Princess Cantacuzene, who was a great feminist, a Swiss lady doctor, the wife of a French general, a Danish missionary, a lady from Greece, and another from Australia.

"Many of the subjects discussed," writes Eiluned Lewis, who has contributed her recollections of the visit,

repeated inevitably India's ever-present themes—poverty, malnutrition, illiteracy, child marriage, problems of the *zenana* and the *harem*, and the wretched conditions among the depressed classes. We heard of fantastic contrasts in the sub-continent, on the one hand the vast, dumb, patient masses of women, many of them still veiled and in complete subjection, and at the other end of the scale a few extremists, demanding equal freedom, equal rights, even the right of divorce.

In between were the courageous, well-informed women gathered from many parts of India and Burma, who came together to consider these matters in those sunlit days of 1936. Dame Elizabeth's long experience of social problems had been in a very different field, but a clear head and a wise heart are international assets. The wholeness of her personality, her direct approach to every problem, the weight of her experience and even the number of her grandchildren, all made a strong appeal to our Indian friends. Whenever she spoke to them it was on the sure ground of humanity.

From Calcutta Elizabeth went north to Lucknow and Agra, visiting the Taj Mahal both by sunlight and by moonlight. "But," says Eiluned Lewis,

it was our day at Fatehpur Sikri which most enchanted us. This rose-red city, built by the Emperor Akbar, has been deserted for hundreds of years and is to-day inhabited only by parrots of brilliant green. The happiness of that day, like the palaces of Akbar, remains untouched by time. I remember Dame Elizabeth's pleasure in a baby's bath of pink marble, set in a garden by the lovely house of Miriam, Akbar's Christian wife, and how—with the help of Murray's *Blue Guide*—we made out the inscription written above the Gate of Victory, which reads, "Jesus, on whom be peace, said the world is a Bridge. Pass over it but build no house on it."

They returned to Delhi, "built beside the ruins of seven previous civilisations," meeting again some of their Indian friends from the Conference and lunching with Lord and Lady Willingdon "amid vice-regal splendours." Then came a short holiday in Rajputana, where the problems of India were momentarily forgotten in the beauty of the countryside.

Life in those ancient Hindu states had stopped still centuries ago, or perhaps moved gently along, no faster than the camel which we met drawing a hansom cab through the streets of Jaipur with an air of dignified disdain.

How we all three enjoyed ourselves! And how nimbly Dame Elizabeth climbed on her elephant for the long ride to the deserted city of Amber. Udaipur, where we stayed in the Maharana's guest house, is surely one of the most beautiful places in the world, a city built of white marble on the shores of a lake. Over this lake we were taken by boat to visit islands where dream-like palaces and their shimmering reflections lay scattered on the water.

On the very day that we were due to leave for Bombay we were invited to attend the Maharana's birthday celebrations, including an elephant fight in the royal courtyard. I am sorry to say that we struggled with our consciences, feeling certain that the trumpeting, trunk-wrestling elephants would be much more of an excitement than a Y.W.C.A. garden party in Bombay, but sorrier still to record that our consciences won, and that we tore ourselves away unwillingly from that Arabian Night existence at the appointed hour.

That last long train journey to Bombay was our final Indian adventure, and brings to mind the endless plains and little sudden hills covered with scrubby jungle, the wild peacocks at dawn feeding on the ground or perched on ancient mud walls, and at every railway station the gaudily clad people of Rajputana with their tin boxes, rolls of bedding and brass pots. But always making her way across the crowded platform, is the upright figure of Dame Elizabeth in her travelling costume of tussore silk, her *terai* hat and her parasol. The memory that I treasure most is a vision of her waving and smiling a good night to me in my upper bunk, her head swathed in a purple silk scarf to keep out the fine red, all-pervading dust.

Two lines from an old hymn have been haunting my mind as I wrote these words,

> And in that Light of life I'll walk
> Till travelling days are done.

Assuredly Dame Elizabeth walked by the "Light of life," and shared its beams with her companions.

It was Elizabeth's belief that to an educated person no country was foreign. She realized the difference in scale of the problems facing the womanhood of India, but she saw them in terms of fundamental human relationships, so that, in the end, they were the same difficult questions with which women at home in

Great Britain were grappling. The need for better and adequate housing, for improved measures of public health, for care for the physical needs of the infant and the school child, for a larger and deeper conception of education for all sections of the community—these were challenges and demands facing the people of Britain and of India alike. The task of women in bringing their influence to bear on the maintenance of peace, in realizing as a living force the common sisterhood that united them beyond all national barriers, were the same throughout the world, East or West. Such was the burden of Elizabeth Cadbury's message to the women of India, and wherever she went she expressed her appreciation of the courage and devotion with which they were facing the work that lay before them, and the record of what had already been achieved by them in the sphere of social reform and of service.

For her the climax came when she was asked to broadcast to the women of India on the subject of International Friendship; the sense of her vast audience, listening unseen, in all parts of that great country was a stimulating experience, the excitement of which she never forgot.

At the end of her stay Margaret Low, the wife of the Editor of the *Times of India* and a leading member of the Indian Council of Women, sent a farewell letter to the boat, as she could not get down to say good-bye in person to Elizabeth.

"Before you go," she wrote,

> I would like to say what a tremendous amount your stay in Bombay has done in cementing friendship between Indian and British women.
>
> I have never seen anyone go straight to their hearts as you have done. They feel that in you they have a sympathetic, understanding friend, and many have said that if there were more visits from you, or from people like you, the misunderstanding between both countries would melt away. . . .
>
> As you are leaving Bombay I would like you to know that you are leaving a multitude of friends, some of whom never had a chance to speak to you, but all of whom feel that they have your understanding and sympathy.

When on the homeward voyage an excursion was arranged from Suez to Cairo, the passengers who went on it rejoining the ship again at Port Said, Elizabeth was well to the fore on this trip, leaving the boat at 6.0 A.M. and returning to it at eleven o'clock at night.

"We visited the Museum at Cairo and saw the marvellous Tutankhamen relics, lunched at Shepheard's, motored to the pyramids and sphinx," she writes to her family.

> Then Mollie and Eiluned mounted on camels, and I on such a swift donkey, that I got back first, and I then wandered round the Mena House Hotel, recalling the visit your father and I made over thirty years ago. Returning to Cairo we had tea on a boat in the river, joined by Mrs Preston, the wife of the High Court Judge at Cairo, whose brother is headmaster of Malvern College. Mrs Preston took me to the new buildings of the Y.W.C.A.; we then visited the citadel, and then back by train to Port Said.

So ended a journey that remained a mountain peak in Elizabeth's range of experience. Her interest in India was maintained throughout the remaining years, and took such practical forms as the gift to the Friends' Mission at Itarsi of a well-equipped travelling dispensary, which could circulate among the outlying villages, and the establishment of a university scholarship for the girls at the Friends' School at Sohagpur. She was a girl of fourteen when Disraeli bestowed the title of Empress of India on Queen Victoria, she was an old lady in her latter eighties when India was granted her freedom by the Labour Government which took office in 1945. The whole troubled chapter of Britain's short-lived Indian Empire was written in her lifetime, and it must have been with satisfaction and renewed hope that she turned the final page.

15

The Challenge of War Renewed

THE years of thought and work, the many miles of travel, the
endless round of committees and discussions, were to prove in
vain. For a second time, at the age of eighty-two, Elizabeth
Cadbury saw her world drift into war; for a second time she met
that challenge by turning her thoughts resolutely to the future
and beginning to plan for the Europe that would succeed the
conflict and its need of social and economic reconstruction.

The Manor Farm was altered and adapted as a training camp
for the Friends' Ambulance Unit, which was revived in 1939,
under the guidance of her great-nephew Paul Cadbury, and
more than a thousand young men passed through it during the
war years. By 1946 the members of the Unit had seen service in
twenty-five different countries in Europe, Asia, and Africa.
Elizabeth Cadbury would pay frequent visits to the young men
in training, chaffing them, seeing that they had at least some
measure of comfort in their spartan surroundings, enjoying their
fun, their stories, their gentle teasing.

As the city she loved and had served for so many long years
was shattered by the night bombing of the Germans, Elizabeth
would sit quietly in the oak-room at the Manor, recalling people
and incidents of the past, resting in unshaken serenity among her
happy memories. Much time was spent by day in tireless
correspondence on behalf of refugees or 'displaced persons' who
had appealed to her for help. Letter after letter was written in
each case to the Foreign Office, the Ministry of Labour, the
refugee organizations, in her efforts to aid these unhappy people
to find a new niche for themselves in the world community.
Money and time were given generously and unsparingly to aid
those cases which her careful investigations proved genuine
and worthy of the effort; whole dossiers of correspondence

remain to witness the conscientious zeal with which she still tried to fulfil her responsibilities to the unfortunate and suffering.

The summer of 1940, which saw the fall of France, brought an unexpected call upon the resources of the Woodlands. A similar hospital in Ostend was ordered to evacuate its premises, and the staff and one hundred and sixty patients, most of them children, arrived at the quayside to find that the boat which was to have taken them off to a port in France had already left. They lay out all night waiting for another boat, and when they got aboard next morning were told that the captain was sailing under secret orders. Not until they were well out at sea did they learn that their destination was England, and not a port in Southern France. When they arrived in England room was found for the children in a hospital in the south, but forty adults, nearly all bed cases, were still without a home. The Matron of the Woodlands received a telephone message—could she accommodate these patients, who would arrive the next day? Somehow it was done—and on a sunny June afternoon Elizabeth was there at the hospital to welcome the forty Belgian invalids, their matron, and three nurses. They quickly settled down into the routine of the English hospital, forming friendships, despite the barriers of language, with English patients and staff; their own matron remained throughout the five years of the war, working happily and harmoniously with Miss Fanny Smith, her English counterpart. It says much for the skill and tact of both women that no word of disagreement, no hint of friction, arose throughout that period. The majority of the patients were nursed back to health, and found work in the locality; some married and settled down in Birmingham. Only one was left as a patient when war ended and the matron could return home.

On the night of November 23, 1940, at 1.0 A.M., the Woodlands was struck by a bomb which destroyed one side of the main house and killed two very valued Sisters while they were having their meal at midnight. Elizabeth notes in her diary that the raids began at seven o'clock on the evening of the twenty-second, and continued through most of the night, with many bombs in the locality of the Manor. A telephone call from the Matron at 7.30 A.M. next day told her of the tragedy which had befallen the hospital, and she was over there shortly afterwards, despite her eighty-two years, "to uphold Matron and her Staff, and go round the wards again, to show our concern for the patients."

"Our own participation at the Manor in the holocaust," she adds, "was broken windows and lack of water and gas. The windows are mended, but we shall have to manage without the services a few days longer." The house of her friends Winifred and Evelyn Sturge, on the Weoley Hill Estate, was shattered, and Winifred Sturge was badly hurt and taken to Selly Oak Hospital. So after her visit to the Woodlands Elizabeth Cadbury set off again to invite Evelyn Sturge to stay at the Manor for the time being and to call on Winifred in hospital, but the former had already gone away, and the latter was quietly sleeping. "Next, I visited Dr Rendel Harris and his tribe to cheer them up," adds the indefatigable old lady, who might well have been in need of comforting and cheering herself after the experiences of that wild night!

The Woodlands did not interrupt its work. Thirty-eight children were sent to the Forelands Hospital at Bromsgrove, and sixty adults returned to their homes, but one hundred and forty remained in the damaged building, and the usual round of hospital life continued. The attitude of the staff was expressed by the imperturbability of the cook, who, with gas and water mains severed, set to work preparing cups of tea for nurses and patients immediately after the explosion, using stoves heated by anthracite, and then remarked, "Well, I may as well sit down for a moment, as it will be time to get breakfast soon." She then produced fried bacon for everybody.

When the war was at last ended it was Elizabeth's great joy in 1946 to fly to Brussels (her first flight, at the age of eighty-eight), with her daughter Dorothea Hoyland, and there meet Lady Nunburnholme, and the Baroness de Poel, President of the International Council of Women, together with representatives of fourteen different countries. Once more they set to work to re-form the International Council, and start again on building the road that would lead to a lasting peace.

"There were representatives of many different countries from

Finland to Czechoslovakia, from Portugal to Greece, each with a different story to tell of terrible privations endured, of difficulties overcome, of achievements won in spite of all," Dorothea Hoyland wrote of this gathering.

Everywhere the National Councils of Women seemed to have been the backbone of every organization that had brought help to the women and children. The Greek Council, for instance, had organized and run two homes for children, in which they had not lost a single child at a time when people were falling dead in the streets from starvation; and those Councils who had had perforce to hibernate during years of occupation seemed to have awakened to a new strength and enthusiasm.

It was a great experience and lovely to see the loving welcome they gave to Mother. The Conference would have missed something very vital if she had not been there, for she helped to forge a link between the old pre-war years and the present. She made them all a charming little speech, telling them how much they had been in all our thoughts during the dark years, and how she had had talks on nearly every country in turn at her International Affairs Committee in London. . . .

When the time came to return home, once more we flew up and up above the clouds into the sunshine beyond, and this seemed symbolic of the experience we had just had, when for a time in meeting so many others working in places far and near for the same causes, we seemed to have pierced through the clouds of doubt and difficulty that often surround us, and had a vision of the new world that might be.

The light of that world shone into the fading eyes of Elizabeth, for her face was set always towards it with gladness and confidence. The weight of years, of disappointments, of disillusionment, the strange, silent loneliness of the very old—none of this could shake her courage, her faith in the possibility of reaching that more gracious and generous life, if men would but submit their search into the hands of God, and follow His leading.

16

The Last Years

THE years had taken wings unto themselves and were slipping by at an astonishing speed. All Elizabeth's children were married and had passed from her immediate care,[1] but there was still so much to do, so many interesting people to meet, old friendships to be maintained and new ones formed, and constantly, it seemed, a fresh group of young people appearing in the family circle, the Bournville Meeting, or the Youth Clubs. The small boys in knickerbockers or little girls in diminutive frocks, children of yesterday, were to-day young men and women concerned with the problem of earning their own livings and finding their footing in the adult world. How was it possible, with the thunder of Time's horses at her heels, for Elizabeth to crowd into the twenty-four hours all that she wished to do before at last she was called upon to lay down her life?

The ten years from eighty to ninety were as rich and full as any of her existence. There was a growing circle of grand-children and great-grandchildren to rejoice in and to come to know, though she once remarked that it did make her feel rather old to be addressed as "great-grandmother." To these newcomers she was the "darling Gran" to whom laboriously written, ill-spelt letters were sent, recording victories won in a prep-school cricket match or tennis tournament, knowing that the joy of the success would be fully shared.

The first arrivals in a new family are naturally always a cause of excitement, but when the fifth or sixth grandchild appeared in the same household it might well be that the grandmother could overlook the event, or send a perfunctory greeting. But Dame Elizabeth, at the age of ninety, arrived in person, with

[1] Laurence to Joyce Mathews in 1925, and Norman to Jeannette Southall in the same year; Ursula, the baby of the family, to Denis Lambert in 1929.

a little coat for her latest small great-granddaughter in this large family, and her own breezy congratulations to the mother, toiling up the stairs to see her in her bedroom and to chuckle over the new arrival.

The range of her interests was as wide as ever. Hampered by her failing eyesight, and in the latter days by a certain loss of hearing, she still continued to keep abreast of the world's doings, the latest ideas in social, political, and religious thought. The last published books lay on her table, and were read to her in the evenings or on train journeys by Elsa Fox, or by any member of the family visiting her. She was still an eager attender at the theatre or at a good film, demanding from her companion a commentary on what was happening when straining eyes and ears failed to deliver their messages. At the end of a day of committees and meetings she would hurry away into Birmingham to attend a concert, and was President of the Birmingham Symphony Orchestra in her ninetieth year. Her interest in the city choir and in the repertory theatre, which she had helped to sponsor from its early days in Birmingham, and her friendship with Sir Barry Jackson remained to the end. It was he who paid a last tribute to her as friend and neighbour in a broadcast talk on the Midland Region after her death. She loved to attend the plays given by the children at the Bournville Schools, or by the dramatic societies at the Works, and the annual children's festival in the village with its maypole and folk-dancing and pageantry.

She had the energy and strength at the age of ninety-two to attend the dinner and reception held to commemorate the founding of Birmingham University, change from her evening clothes in a room provided for her at the University, and motor up to London during the night, so that after a few hours' rest at her Club she might be present at the Meeting for Sufferings in the morning.

She was the President of the United Nations Association in Bournville, and took a keen interest in all its meetings. In June 1948 she attended a reception at Downing Street, given by the Prime Minister for presidents and representatives of this body, meeting a great many people she knew, and coming away full of hope, in spite of all the difficulties, for the work of the United Nations in keeping the peace of the world.

The future policies and plans of the Liberal Party were still watchfully followed and commented upon, and she became a vice-president of the Liberal Federation. The great Socialist victory in 1945 she was prepared to meet with a careful, open-minded consideration, and the reminder to her family that if the people in office would do fairly by the poor and the underdog it mattered little by which party the good was done.

When, under the new Education Act, the older children from the Bournville Village Schools were dispersed to various senior schools in the city's environs, Elizabeth Cadbury made a point of visiting every child in the new surroundings, to see that each was happy and settling down satisfactorily. One of the hardest things for her to accept under the changing order of society was that Bournville could not have its own senior school[1] so that after the age of eleven the children had to be removed from the familiar setting of the village, to continue their education elsewhere.

The needs of the displaced persons, whose homes had been engulfed by the sweep of political tides in Central and Eastern Europe were ever-present in her thoughts. Her efforts for their resettlement in different lands and new callings were steady and persistent throughout her latter years.

"One of our refugee boys, G. K., now naturalised and in the British Army, paid us a visit on Saturday," she wrote in a letter of February 1946:

One of our Czech correspondents who is now free after six years of prison wrote to tell us how the letters and memories of his English friends was the one thing to which he clung during the years he was in Buchenwald. Another letter I have had is from a refugee whose mother, a Russian subject, was in Rome during the war and unable to come to him in England, though we had been trying to get a permit for her. The son is doing well in a job in Devonshire, and I guaranteed her reliability and her maintenance, and a week ago we had an ecstatic letter saying that she had at last arrived at Southampton and he was taking her to his Devonshire home. Some of these happier touches relieve my often harassing correspondence.

The cry of these distressed and suffering people, with their

[1] One is now being built and, it is understood, will bear Elizabeth Cadbury's name.

M

broken and divided families, their hopelessness, or their un-yielding courage, was never forgotten. Elizabeth Cadbury felt their need as a heavy burden of responsibility laid upon her, which, by her nature, she could not escape.

All her multifarious interests were maintained, and she was always slipping away to London to attend the meetings of the National and International Council of Women, the National Peace Council, a Y.W.C.A. Executive, the Friends' Service Council (which sponsored the international and missionary service of the Society of Friends), or the executive committee of the Society, the Meeting for Sufferings, held each month. Her crisp, incisive comments in committees, her gift of making the brief, appropriate speech with grace and humour on any occasion when she was called upon to speak, remained with her to the last. She always had the ability to seize on the essential points of a subject under discussion, and to clarify a confused situation by putting these essentials in a few cogent sentences. Whether she were giving the chief address at a school speech-day, or talking to her Adult School women in a Bible class, chairing a public meeting in the Town Hall of Birmingham, or presiding over a hospital committee—she brought not merely an intellectual grasp of her subject, but the wide range of her own vision to give her listeners a sense of the possibilities ahead for the man or woman of faith and imagination.

Elizabeth Cadbury remained Chairman of the Bournville Village Trust till her death, and her enthusiasm and eagerness to provide the homes so much needed after the War, particularly for young people, never waned. She was exasperated by delays, by red tape, by unimaginative officialdom, and spoke her mind bluntly. It was a red-letter day when she opened the two-hundredth post-war house built on the estate in 1950, at the Jubilee Celebrations in the village, and, despite the rain, scorned the umbrella offered for her protection at this ceremony. Her contact with the Girls' and Youths' Clubs of the Bournville Works was unbroken; in 1950, at the age of ninety-two, she would appear on a wild and stormy winter's night at a Youth Club play, when many had feared that the weather would daunt anyone of her advanced years. But those who knew her

best averred that she would come if she had promised, and
proved to be right. She sometimes entertained the representatives
of the firm at the Manor, and a particularly happy gathering of
their wives in 1951 brought to many a sense of her personal interest
and friendship for all who were connected with the business.

There were new interests also to absorb time and energy.
Sir Francis Younghusband enlisted her help in his inauguration
of a World Congress of Faiths which should bring the followers
of different religions into a closer fellowship and understanding
of one another. She presided at the opening meeting of the
Congress in the Queen's Hall in 1936, and it was in July 1942,
while he was staying as a guest at the Manor and attending a
gathering of the Congress in Birmingham, that Sir Francis was
stricken with his mortal illness.

Her own spartan habits were unabated; in her ninetieth year
she still took a cold bath every morning, and in the last, wet and
chilly summer of her life she persisted in bathing while staying
by the sea at Weston-super-Mare. Every night, before going
to bed, however long and tiring the day had been, she would
go out for a walk round her house, beneath the stars, or in rain
or snow, and then come in to sleep freshened and quietened
by that quarter of an hour of solitude, alone with the winds and
the clouds and her sense of the presence of God.

The crowning point of those last strenuous happy years was
reached on Elizabeth Cadbury's ninetieth birthday on June 24,
1948. At seven o'clock the strains of a hymn sung outside her
bedroom door by her three daughters, an old custom of their
childhood, aroused Elizabeth Cadbury, and she woke appropri-
ately to the sound of the words,

> Summer suns are glowing
>   Over land and sea;
> Happy light is flowing
>   Bountiful and free,
> Everything rejoices
>   In the mellow rays;
> All earth's thousand voices
>   Swell the psalm of praise.

From breakfast-time onward groups of her friends and official
deputations from the city, the Bournville Works and Village,

the Youth Clubs and Hospitals, the Friends' Meeting and the Selly Oak Colleges, came pouring up the drive in the brilliant June sunshine with their greetings and gifts. Erect, gracious, glowing with happiness, Dame Elizabeth stood on the terrace to receive the visitors, with a kindly, pertinent, or witty rejoinder to each little speech of congratulation. When the Warden of Woodbrooke suggested that now she had achieved her ninetieth year she might consider entering the College as a student, she replied instantly: "No, I shall wait until I am a hundred, and then I shall come as a Fellow."

In the afternoon a party was held for her at "The Davids," the home of Laurence and Joyce Cadbury on the opposite side of the Bristol road to the Manor House. Here nearly one hundred and fifty near relatives of Dame Elizabeth were gathered, including thirty-eight of her grandchildren and thirty-four of her great-grandchildren. She moved among them all, serene and light-hearted, joking and laughing with infectious gaiety with her youngest descendants, talking of old times and friendships with her cousins and nephews and nieces. At six o'clock, when most of the guests were preparing to depart, a little jaded with the festivities and excitement and the summer heat, Elizabeth, brisk as ever, announced that she must, unfortunately, hurry away to attend a meeting at the Queen Elizabeth Hospital. It had been arranged to hold the final meeting that evening of the Governors and Staffs of the United Hospitals before they were taken over by the State as part of the National Health Service. "As President for several years I felt I ought to attend. The date had been fixed to suit the Lord Mayor, and it could not be altered when it was discovered that it was rather a special day for me. However, we had a very good gathering and I had to make a sort of wind-up speech as well as take part in the meeting, after which we retired for refreshments and speculative talks with regard to the future."

Her daughter Dorothea Hoyland, writing of the birthday afterwards, said that it would have been impossible to imagine anything more happy; the deep impression left upon her was the spontaneity and sincerity of the expressions of love and admiration and gratitude that came pouring in all day.

"I do not think any family could have had such a free and adventurous childhood to look back upon and so many happy memories," wrote another daughter, Mollie. "It is difficult to express one's thoughts and feelings about the events of yesterday, but emerging above everything else is the note of affection and thankfulness from such a tremendous and varied number of friends for thee, and for thy wonderful life of thought for others —no word of personal success except in relation to achievement in a public cause."

"The party was such a wonderfully happy occasion that I am sure all ages, young and old, enjoyed it enormously," wrote her son-in-law Bertram Crosfield. "But above all, the gathering was a small tribute to what we all owe to you as the head of the family. You are so much more than the oldest member, or the apex of the arch. You are a real inspiration and encouragement to us to make the most of our lives. . . . I am so glad that the fourth generation are able to catch some of that inspiration from you at first hand."

"I thought you were simply marvellous dashing round and talking to everyone and then going off to a hospital meeting at the end of it," wrote a schoolgirl granddaughter.

A grandson in Canada, George Woodall Cadbury, who in his young manhood had reacted against the Cadbury wealth and expressed extreme socialist views, summed up the feeling of the younger people, both within and without her family circle.

I always felt that you and I were the youngest members of the Bournville Village Trust, and as the one who tended to be the young radical amongst the whole group, I could always count on your interest and very often your support for a new idea, and that is a pretty wonderful situation when there is a whole generation between us.

Her American cousin, Rufus Jones, whom Elizabeth had helped in one of his darkest hours, dictated a letter from his sick-bed to express his love and his appreciation of her years of devoted life and service. He did not live through the night to sign it, and it was finished by his wife and daughter. Elizabeth kept it among her most treasured possessions, marked 'very special.'

A son-in-law, Geoffrey Hoyland, sending his love and congratulations before the birthday, said that he knew she would be snowed under with messages from all quarters congratulating her on the wonderful achievements of a wonderful life, "but only those who have lived close to thee can know that thy greatest achievement of all is just thyself, and it is for that that we give thanks." The questions posed by the Percy Bigland portrait, painted forty years before, were answered. The years had brought not querulousness and a growing love of domination, but a mellowing, a softening of the harsher outlines, a ripening wisdom to curb the swift impatience, the imperious will, the dangerous satisfactions of power. They had brought a growing tolerance, the capacity to compromise when it was a matter of wishes rather than principle, a new, steady patience which helped those of more limited vision to stumble slowly along the paths of a wider thinking. Impetuous, generous, hasty, Elizabeth had maintained throughout an inner sincerity, a simplicity of heart and faith, a trust and delight in people and in the small joys of daily living, that brought her not only the respect and admiration of those she encountered, but their love.

In November 1948 the first break in the family of eleven occurred with the death of Edward Cadbury, who had been ailing for many months. Elizabeth Cadbury felt keenly the loss of her eldest stepson, whose counsel on the Bournville Village Trust she had always greatly valued, and on whom she had come to rely for many things since the death of her own husband. But her first thought was not of her own sorrow and bereavement, but of the wife, Dorothy, who was left behind to face the bitter loneliness. In the following weeks Elizabeth spent much time with her, by the mere fact of her own vital personality and presence bringing courage to meet the days ahead.

She was called upon also in those last years of her life to face the deaths, in their young manhood, of two grandsons with whom she had a special friendship. Patrick, the second son of Egbert Cadbury, fell from his bedroom window while walking in his sleep on a summer night of 1941, and Julian, the eldest son of Laurence, was killed in a motor accident when on holiday in France in July 1950. Again, in the bitterness of her personal sorrow, Elizabeth Cadbury's first concern was to summon all her resources of strength that she might comfort and fortify the parents in the first dark hours of loss.

A great and happy culmination of her long years of service to Bournville came in the midsummer of 1951, when the Village celebrated its jubilee. Dame Elizabeth moved among the crowds that week, which began on her ninety-third birthday, supremely happy and content to see the development of her husband's work, to witness the joyful affection with which she was greeted. The children thronged about her car, waving and cheering, giving her a truly royal reception whenever she appeared. A Jubilee Exhibition was held in the thirteenth-century house, Minworth Greaves, which had been bought by the Trust in 1911 and erected piece by piece on the Village Green to save it from destruction. The Exhibition was opened by the Lord Mayor of Birmingham, who paid tribute in his speech to the memory of the great pioneer, George Cadbury. At the children's festival on the Saturday the biggest crowds in the history of the Village collected on the Green. Over a thousand children sat down to tea, and afterwards Elizabeth distributed prizes among them. She was back again later in the evening to see the firework display, provided by the Cadbury firm, and amid the bursting stars, the flaming comet trails of the rockets, the week of festivity came to an end.

It was to prove Elizabeth's last public appearance, a fitting close, for as she walked among the realized dreams of the past she was still looking to the future, and to the building of a new generation of Bournville citizens.

17

The Closing of a Chapter

AFTER only a few weeks of restricted activity and failing health, on the night of December 4, 1951, Elizabeth Cadbury passed from this world in the hours of peaceful sleeping. Her mind was still filled with plans and purposes to be accomplished in the days ahead—Christmas festivities for the grandchildren, a meeting of the Friends Essay Society, which she greatly desired should meet once more at the Manor, the twenty-first birthday of a granddaughter, the Bournville Schools' Christmas Party, the Women's Adult School at Severn Street and its particular needs at the Christmas season. She attended the Friends' Meeting at Bournville a week before her death and paid a last visit to her beloved Bournville Schools only a few hours before unconsciousness stole upon her. A month before, when saying good-bye to a member of the family after a visit, she had said, "I want you always to think of me walking up the garden into the sunshine"; and death found her already looking beyond the rain and fogs of that grey Midland winter to the days of spring and the upsurge of new life with a glad expectancy. These are typical memories of her, and of her courage and hope.

The Manor must have seemed strangely empty in those last years of her life, though she had given the upper storey as sleeping quarters to the student nurses at the Woodlands who were short of accommodation. She saw little of them in their coming and going, but it gave her a sense of satisfaction that there were still young people in the house. She lived on the two lower floors, tended with devoted care by Elsa Fox, her constant companion for the last twenty years of her life, and at times by Elsa's sister, Anna. Miss Phyllis Cook carried out her secretarial duties, taking the burden of her heavy daily correspondence from Elizabeth's shoulders; she was still served by maids of long

standing, very specially by the faithful Annie Somers, who had
come first as parlour maid to the house at Wind's Point. Tutton,
her chauffeur, drove her from committee to committee, from
Birmingham to London or to the Malvern Hills, and took upon
himself a multitude of small jobs and services for the depleted
household. Yet, with all this care and thoughtfulness surrounding
her, the big, shadowy rooms lacked the noise and movement,
the laughter, the battles, and the joyousness of the family life
that had once filled them to overflowing. It is not surprising that
in the last evenings of her life they were often peopled for her
by the presence of absent children or of brothers and sisters
long dead, who had come to spend happy weeks in her home.
The years and the generations blended and blurred, and time
with its divisions was meaningless. So as she paced the corridors
of her house Elizabeth was serenely happy in her sense of the
presence of those whom she had loved most. And death came
gently as a friend to release her from the limitations of a body
grown at last frail and tired.

Tributes to her life and service filled the Press in the days
following her death. Messages of sympathy came pouring in
from all four quarters of the British Isles and from many parts
of the world. From Queen Mary, who sent a telegram mourning
the passing of "my very dear old friend," to the small, unknown
child who laid a solitary flower tied with a piece of ribbon among
the posies brought to the Bournville Meeting House, the sense
of personal loss was vivid and equally shared.

Two memorial services were held in her remembrance:
one, a smaller gathering of relatives and intimate friends at the
Bournville Village Meeting House on December 7, which took
the form of a Quaker Meeting for Worship; the other, a public
service in one of the large dining-rooms of the Bournville
Works on December 16, when more than 2500 people came
together to render her a last act of homage. All classes, all shades
of political opinion, and nearly all branches of the Christian
faith were represented in that congregation. Lord Justice Birkett
gave the address, drawing on his long years of friendship with
Elizabeth Cadbury to recall her personality and her ceaselessly
active life. Linking the names of George and Elizabeth Cadbury,

N

because "they are inseparably joined together," he emphasized that:

> For thirty years after that association ended, Dame Elizabeth carried on the private and public work they had together in-augurated, with the same practical idealism, the same vision, the same zeal, and the same complete devotion to the public and private good. Of both of them it must be said, however, that whilst they will be remembered for what they did, they will like-wise be remembered for what they were. High purpose is the badge of the great man or woman. . . . George and Elizabeth Cadbury were great in purpose and great in achievement; but it was nevertheless a greatness of heart and mind that created the high purpose, and made all that marvellous outward achievement possible.

It was not the forceful public speaker, the able organizer, the bold leader along untried paths of thought and action, who had brought together the large congregation on that Sunday afternoon in December. It was Elizabeth Cadbury, the woman, as she was, the friend who came in the hour of suffering with a sure word of strength and comfort, or who was miraculously there at a moment of great need with some practical offer of help, some vision of the way forward; it was the mother who never failed a child in a moment of conflict and doubt and grief, the grand-mother who knew and understood the joys and the fears of early childhood, who was remembered and honoured that day.

Public recognition of her services came to her in the number of orders and decorations awarded during the last quarter of her life. She was made an Officer of the Order of the British Empire in 1918, and created a Dame Commander of the Order in 1934. The Order of Queen Elizabeth of the Belgians and that of the Belgian Officier de Couronne were presented to her at the close of the first World War in recognition of her work for the refugees; Serbian and Greek Red Cross awards and the Order of St Sava of Yugoslavia and of an Officer of the Hospital of St John of Jerusalem followed in grateful memory of her services to the stricken people of those countries.

Though she received these awards with a childlike pleasure, she made little parade of them. It was the honour brought to the family name she bore rather than to herself as a person that counted with her. Most of the time the dignities and titles were forgotten, genuinely forgotten, overlaid by her many interests— in people as individuals, in possibilities of further work for her community and her age, in her anticipation of the opportunities offered by the future to the courageous and the young in heart.

With children she maintained a direct and frank relationship, neither sentimental nor condescending. They were people to be considered in their own right, treated with courtesy, friendliness, and dignity. To one enthusiast in committee who was extolling the value of nursery schools for every child indiscriminately, on the plea that children delighted only in the companionship of their contemporaries, Dame Elizabeth remarked crisply that she entirely disagreed with the last speaker. Nothing was more wholesome for a child than to learn to meet happily with adults also. If the Almighty had intended children only to enjoy the friendship of those of their own age he would doubtless have arranged for them to be born in litters!

To the end her faith in youth, her sympathy with its needs and aspirations, remained undimmed. The modern young men and women might be different in many ways from those of her own generation. But, she insisted, they were only different, and not in any way inferior, as many older people seemed to believe. The world and its methods had radically changed, and the demand made upon youth was not only that it must keep abreast of the times, but that it should break new trails. To do this, young people would rightly ask for more freedom and independence. Courage and a spirit of adventure had always been part of the make-up of the young and should be given free play. What Elizabeth Cadbury also asked of the coming generation was the patience to acquire knowledge, to build up sound powers of judgment, not merely to rest content with the material and physical benefits that an age of discovery and invention had conferred upon them, but to remember the need to look beyond the things temporal to the things eternal if they were to find the strength to weather triumphantly the storms of their age.

The essence of the life that she longed to see evoked in the children and the youth of her city and her country was not a

matter of formal religious instruction or the non-sectarian
scripture lesson of the State schools. It was too elusive and intangible to be influenced or developed in such ways. It came,
she maintained, chiefly from "the appreciation of the immanence
of the Divine in daily life and in common things"; from the
perception of that power which can transform the often
monotonous and humdrum claims of daily life, and make of
them a thing of beauty. Was it not the secret that she herself
had discovered, the source of the strength and untiring energy
that carried her through the long years of service to her community and her age?

Her counsel to young people about to embark on marriage
was pungent with humour and a salty common sense: "It is
when a man gives his wife the butcher's money with the air of
bestowing a valuable birthday gift, that the wife feels like
'kicking,'" she remarked, quoting from an article she had read.

"A man who is late for his train won't observe the rules of debate.
Your best plan is to concentrate on getting him off. Similarly, if
his shoe-lace breaks, or he loses his collar-stud, don't feel aggrieved
if he vents his wrath on you. A man who has lost his stud has
ceased to be a rational being. The remedy is to have a new one to
hand."

To these dicta she added her own advice.

Put a spice of humour into the matrimonial mixture. Many people
regard marriage as a shouldering of new responsibilities; they
prepare for it as for a battle.

Never have any financial secrets from each other. We have both
got funny little habits, but we won't call attention to them when
visitors are present. No arguments at breakfast, or before any
other meals. Don't forget anniversaries. Never worry about what
other people (this includes relations) say and think. We haven't
married them. Hold fast to the ideals of courtship days. Don't
drag up the past. Bury the hatchet, but don't mark its grave.

It was her care for the small, intimate details of family life
and of personal relationships that was the secret of Elizabeth
Cadbury's success as a mother and head of a household, as
employer and friend.

That personal touch which could withstand the rubs of daily

life and work, and could draw into her own enthusiasms and interests those who served her, was Elizabeth Cadbury's supreme gift. It was this that enabled her to keep the needs and desires of individuals before her in her larger schemes for the social and international betterment of the world. She never lost sight of the person in the intricacies of the design. To all her work she brought the powers of a fresh and active mind, illogical at moments, unwise at moments in her judgments and decisions, but always stimulating, provocative, humorous.

"She never rested on her oars or stood still in thought," wrote Miss M. M. Sharples, who had been a colleague of Elizabeth Cadbury for many years in the National and International Councils of Women.

"And still, amidst the crashing of the old world-orders, her work goes on, for it belongs to the things that are eternal. Forms pass, nations come and go, creeds and customs alter . . . but the great human attributes of freedom, tolerance, and peace for which she has worked so untiringly are part of the immortal heritage of the spirit of man."

The years had gone, ninety-three of them, since Elizabeth Cadbury first opened her eyes on the changing world of the mid-Victorian Age. She had lived through some of the most rapid changes in technical achievement, in thought, in social structure, that had ever been witnessed. For in the course of that lifetime she had passed from the gas-lit capital of the horse-drawn carriage and the hansom cab, to the London of neon lights and the motor-car, to the world of the luxury liner and the aeroplane, of wireless and television and radar, and the split atom, with all its immense potentialities for good or evil in the lives of men and nations. She had watched the girl of the middle-classes emerge slowly from schoolroom and drawing-room, where she had learned a smattering of polite and trivial accomplishments, to take her place as a comrade, competitor, and responsible citizen alongside her male contemporaries, carving her way in every profession, entering Parliament, striking out her own ideas and following freely where they led.

Elizabeth Cadbury had struggled for the abolition of slumdom, of ignorance, and malnutrition, and had witnessed the first

tentative steps taken in this country in housing and health and
public elementary education. She lived to see the rise of the
Social Welfare State, the restriction and redistribution of income,
the beginning of the battle with new dangers of totalitarianism
and of a dull level of mediocrity. She had followed the revolu-
tions of thought in science, in religion, in politics, which had
overthrown the old faith in an inevitable progress, in the gradual
advance of mankind on the road to perfectibility, in unquestioning acceptance of the authority of the Bible. In their place had
come the doubts and disillusionment brought by the experience
of two world wars, a series of question marks written across the
old certainties, the collapse of many standards of value which
had guided her generation in youth and middle age. She had
met and entertained many of the leading men and women of
different generations who were fashioning the thought and
directing the activities of the country—statesmen and historians,
politicians and industrialists, social welfare workers and teachers,
clergy, and ministers, scientists and playwrights. It was Bernard
Shaw, the great sceptic, who said of her that "if there is a
life after this, she is one of the very few people I would like to
meet there." Though her wealth had removed her from the
common cares of financial stress and the struggle to make ends
meet, she had the sympathy and imagination to realize in generous
measure the worries and mental suffering of those less fortunate,
and never forgot the responsibilities her fortune laid upon her.
She met pain and physical disability with a high-hearted courage
that refused to be daunted by the limitations they imposed. After
her sight had failed she once remarked that if she had not been a
Christian she would have taken her own life. It is a sudden,
revealing touch of what the growing darkness cost her. She had
known many times the despair of loss as, one by one, those she
had loved and honoured slipped away before her into the silence
of death. Now, at the very end of her days, some one asked
Elizabeth what it had all meant to her, what she had learned
from life. The answer, in her own words, is the inevitable and
fitting conclusion to this book:

As I look back down the long years I note what wonderful
opportunities have opened out before me, bringing experience,

adventure, inspiring friendships and new enterprises, some crowned with success, others bringing disappointments; the happiness of family life, anxieties and experiments in the training of children, the rejoicing as one sees them becoming helpful and cultivated citizens, their fresh and youthful search after truth. Then the discoveries of so much that is good in the world to set against the evil has been so enheartening. The help and inspiration that comes by association with great minds, and devoted workers in every class in life, in every nationality; the pleasure of living with, working with, speculating with those who, in the midst of earnest endeavour bring joy, humour, patience, faith into everyday life.

If you say "Would you like to repeat your life?" I would say, "Yes, if all the splendid people I have known could do the same."

Index

Bournville Factory (*see* Cadbury Brothers Limited), Girls' and Youths' Clubs at, 112, 114, 115, 134, 135, 136, 140, 178 ; Friends Meeting at, 69

Bournville Schools:
Adult, 69
children's party, 184
Day Continuation, 110
Ruskin Hall, 99
Sunday, 99, 128
village, 101, 128, 177; becomes Chairman of Committee of, 111

Bournville Village and Estate (*see also* Bournville Schools, *and* Bournville Village Trust):
children's festival, 183
'company village,' not a, 136
foundation of, 47; helps George Cadbury in, 74
Friends' Meeting, 69, 70, 102, 148, 153, 185
German Burgomasters visit, 92
growth of, 136
Public Utility Societies, 135
royal visit to, 134
tenants, relations with, 75
town planning, influence on, 94

Bournville Village Trust (*see also above, and* Cadbury, George), 18, 74, 87, 91, 148; becomes Chairman of, 135, 178; jubilee of, 178, 183

Bowley (Cash), Elizabeth (aunt), 17

Boys' classes in London, conducts, 31, 33

Bradley (Manor House), 56

Braithwaite, William Charles, 95, 96, 97

Brayshaw, A. Neave, 99

Bright, John, 9, 19

British Museum Reading Room, reads at, 27

Broadcasts, 145, 150

de Broen, Mlle, 34

Brook House, 94 *n.*, 136

Brown, F. M., 97

Browning, 40, 41

Brussels, visits, 162, 173

Bryan, Tom, 99, 100

Bunhill Fields, works at, 35, 51

Burns, John, 73, 92

Buss, Miss, 25

CADBURY BROTHERS LIMITED, 87, 110, 119, 136

Cadbury Family:
Barrow (nephew), 92, 113 *n.*; Mrs (Dame Geraldine), 113
Dorothea (Mrs G. Hoyland) (daughter), 54 *n.*, 58, 62, 63 *n.*, 99 *n.*, 119, 122, 123, 131, 134, 149, 173, 180
Edward (stepson), 48, 63 *n.*, 70 *n.*, 86 *n.*, 114, 118 *n.*
Egbert (son), 54 *n.*, 63 *n.*, 123, 130, 182; Patrick (grandson), 182
Eleanor (Mrs B. Crosfield) (step-daughter), 48, 63 *n.*, 94, 118 *n.*, 119
Elizabeth Mary ("Elsie" Taylor), *passim*
George, George and Elizabeth— *see below*
George (junior) (stepson), 48, 51, 58, 63 *n.*, 100, 108, 110 118 *n.*
George Woodall (grandson), 181
Henry (stepson), 48, 51, 63 *n.*, 64, 86 *n.*, 118 *n.*, 132, 146 and *n.*
Isabel (Mrs K. Wilson) (step-daughter), 48, 51, 54, 63 *n.*, 94, 118 *n.*
Jessie (niece), 49
John (father of George Cadbury), 46, 49
Laurence (son), 54 and *n.*, 63 *n.*, 79, 123, 175 *n.*, 180, 183; Mrs Laurence, 79, 180; Julian (grandson), 182
Marion (Mrs W. E. Greeves) (daughter), 54 and *n.*, 58, 63 *n.*, 122, 123, 130, 165, 170, 181
Mary. *See* Tylor
Norman (son), 54 *n.*, 63 *n.*, 120, 123, 175 *n.*
Paul, 171
Richard (brother-in-law), 45, 49, 61, 69, 71, 87